T0334139

Cambridge Elements ≡

Elements in Twenty-First Century Music Practice
edited by
Simon Zagorski-Thomas
London College of Music, University of West London

SHARED LISTENINGS

Methods for Transcultural Musicianship and Research

Stefan Östersjö
Luleå University of Technology

Nguyễn Thanh Thủy
Royal College of Music in Stockholm

David G. Hebert
Western Norway University of Applied Sciences

Henrik Frisk
Royal College of Music in Stockholm

CAMBRIDGE
UNIVERSITY PRESS

CAMBRIDGE
UNIVERSITY PRESS

Shaftesbury Road, Cambridge CB2 8EA, United Kingdom

One Liberty Plaza, 20th Floor, New York, NY 10006, USA

477 Williamstown Road, Port Melbourne, VIC 3207, Australia

314–321, 3rd Floor, Plot 3, Splendor Forum, Jasola District Centre,
New Delhi – 110025, India

103 Penang Road, #05–06/07, Visioncrest Commercial, Singapore 238467

Cambridge University Press is part of Cambridge University Press & Assessment,
a department of the University of Cambridge.

We share the University's mission to contribute to society through the pursuit of
education, learning and research at the highest international levels of excellence.

www.cambridge.org
Information on this title: www.cambridge.org/9781009462259

DOI: 10.1017/9781009272575

First published 2023

A catalogue record for this publication is available from the British Library

ISBN 978-1-009-46225-9 Hardback
ISBN 978-1-009-27254-4 Paperback
ISSN 2633-4585 (online)
ISSN 2633-4577 (print)

Shared Listenings

Methods for Transcultural Musicianship and Research

Elements in Twenty-First Century Music Practice

DOI: 10.1017/9781009272575
First published online: September 2023

Stefan Östersjö
Luleå University of Technology

Nguyễn Thanh Thủy
Royal College of Music in Stockholm

David G. Hebert
Western Norway University of Applied Sciences

Henrik Frisk
Royal College of Music in Stockholm

Author for correspondence: Stefan Östersjö, stefan.ostersjo@ltu.se

Abstract: This Element demonstrates how a combination of stimulated recall and collaborative autoethnographic strategies can be applied to artistic and scholarly work at the intersection of ethnomusicology and practice-led-research. The authors relate recently collected material from fieldwork in Vietnam to the long-term method development within the Vietnamese/Swedish group The Six Tones, of which three authors are the founding members. The discussion centers around the inter-subjective forms of stimulated recall analysis, developed through the creative work of this innovative intercultural music ensemble. The aim of this project is to create a decolonized methodology—for both music performance and research—and it provides a detailed account of this method development starting in 2006. Furthermore, the authors discuss how this practice was successfully shared with three master performers in the south of Vietnam as part of a collaborative project in 2018–2019.

This Element has a video abstract, available at Cambridge.org/Östersjö_abstract

Keywords: Intercultural music, stimulated recall, ethnomusicology, artistic research, decolonisation

ISBNs: 9781009462259 (HB), 9781009272544 (PB), 9781009272575 (OC)
ISSNs: 2633-4585 (online), 2633-4577 (print)

Contents

1 Introduction

Shared listenings may initially seem a familiar practice as one imagines a typical social situation with friends, together experiencing the power of music. In this Element, we are interested in what happens to the listening experience when shared understanding cannot be taken for granted. How can musicians learn to listen for the unexpected in transcultural encounters? We propose that intercultural musicianship and transcultural musical understanding may be built on the grounds of such shared listening, which stretches beyond what Judith Becker (2010) discusses as a habitus of listening.

This publication takes us on a journey through an array of illuminating experiences and even discoveries made within the context of The Six Tones, an ensemble, which was formed to explore intercultural collaboration between musicians from Vietnam and Sweden. The group was established in 2006 when the Vietnamese *đàn tranh*[1] player Nguyễn Thanh Thủy (coauthor of this Element) and *đàn bầu*[2] player Ngô Trà My were guest teachers in the traditional music programs at the Malmö Academy of Music.[3] There, they first met Swedish guitarist Stefan Östersjö and composer and improviser Henrik Frisk (who were PhD students at the same institution). Through experimental workshops, encounters between traditional Vietnamese and contemporary Western music were created.[4] A fundamental building block in the creation of the group was the idea of mutual learning, based on the ideal of creating space for equal contribution to all levels of decision-making as well as artistic initiative. It was obvious at the outset that this would entail negotiating musical meaning across

---

[1] The *đàn tranh* is a plucked zither from Vietnam, similar to the Chinese *guzheng*, the Japanese *koto*, the Korean *kayagum*, and the Mongolian *yatga*. It has a long sound box with steel strings, movable bridges, and tuning pegs positioned on the top.

[2] The *đàn bầu* is a Vietnamese monochord. Its basic playing technique relies on harmonics, the pitch of which is modulated by shifting the basic pitch of the string. It is an instrument that perfectly embodies the fundamental building blocks of traditional Vietnamese music and allows the performer a wide range of ornamental figurations and vibrati.

[3] Their work in the Malmö Academy of Music was funded through a long-term exchange program by the Swedish International Development Cooperation Agency (SIDA), running between 2000 and 2010. As leading performers on the traditional music scenes and teachers in the Vietnam National Academy of Music, Nguyễn Thanh Thủy and Ngô Trà My were invited for repeated residency periods often three to four months at a time. In a book chapter (2014) Nguyễn Thanh Thủy reflects on her experience of teaching traditional music to Swedish students. The SIDA project also became the source of funding for the continued work of the group until 2009, when they embarked on their first artistic research project, titled (re)thinking Improvisation.

[4] The four of us worked for two days, eventually producing material for two works, one for ten-string guitar and electronics, and a quartet titled "The Six Tones," which we premiered in a concert in Hà Nội in October of the same year. In a rooftop restaurant, celebrating that concert with a majestic view over Hoàn Kiếm lake in the old town in Hà Nội, we decided to establish our ensemble as a long-term project and to call it The Six Tones. Our group's name came from the piece we had just premiered, which in turn referred to how the six tones of the Vietnamese language also form a foundation for Vietnamese music, by guiding the shape of melodic lines.

different musical systems, a fact that challenged conventional listening and also launched many creative processes. Consider, for instance, the difference between conventional Western tonality and the modal system of Vietnamese music, where fundamental musical expressions such as those defining *cheerful* or *sad* are related not to the organization of pitch and harmony but rather for the most part to the type of ornamentation characterizing the expression of each mode (Lê, 2003).

Already in the first working sessions, Nguyễn Thanh Thủy and Ngô Trà My had embarked on a journey toward mastering sound worlds of experimental music and of developing novel techniques to make these speak through traditional Vietnamese instruments, as expressed in a Skype conversation in summer 2008 between Östersjö and Nguyễn:

> Thủy: I seem to be very aware of what is perceived as "Vietnamese" in my playing. I believe I was myself quite constantly aware of this difference when we worked.
>
> Stefan: It seems to me that the perception of this difference is also projected from outside, your identity as a performer when playing to a Western audience appears to be built on the expectations from the audience on this "otherness."
>
> Thủy: That is different today. I think I am not as concerned with the expectations on my being Vietnamese when I play to an audience outside of Vietnam. In fact, instead I seem to more often reflect on how my playing is changing; now it seems to be less and less shaped by my background in traditional music. (Östersjö & Nguyễn, 2013, p. 190)

Meanwhile, Östersjö had started to develop techniques for emulating the sound of the *đàn tranh* and the *đàn bầu* on his own instruments, which in turn enabled adaptations of traditional Vietnamese music for hybrid settings within the group. A process of mutual learning had begun.

Our intention with this publication is to seek an understanding of how such intercultural learning unfolds and eventually transforms the embodied knowledge of a musician.[5] Intercultural music-making is challenging, not the least to the listening habits of participating musicians. By engaging in intercultural collaboration we have all come to see how our listening is both embodied and socioculturally situated. At the same time we have come to see our listening as a gate to approaching the Other, and this Element seeks to describe some of the methods that have shaped such shared listenings.

---

[5] In a video essay, titled *The (re)Turn*, Nguyễn Thanh Thủy interviewed Stefan Östersjö about approaches to intercultural collaboration in The Six Tones (Nguyễn, 2022), which forms part of an exposition in the VIS journal. This video essay may serve as an introduction to the artistic methods of the group: www.researchcatalogue.net/view/1513023/1513024.

While referring to The Six Tones as a case, a holistic aim of this Element is to develop an understanding of how music research can be grounded in listening. The Six Tones have been part of a series of artistic research[6] projects, the first, (re)thinking Improvisation, starting in 2009. In 2012 the group embarked on a second project, Music in Movement, which explored how gesture could be a means for analytical approaches to music performance. This entailed specific attention to gendered gestures (Nguyễn, 2019) and their culturally situated nature and also artistic explorations of the potential for creating music wherein performed gesture served as compositional material (Östersjö, 2016). Through this series of projects – of which Musical Transformations (2018–22), funded by the Swedish Marcus and Amalia Wallenberg Foundation, is central to the present publication – we have sought to develop methods for intersubjective knowledge formation in music through the use of "stimulated recall." As an analytical practice in music research, we find this method central since it uses sonic materials as data, and the analysis can be carried out through listening. However, a particular focus in designing methods for the study of intercultural collaboration – when the listening is not immediately shared – is the negotiation of an intersubjective understanding across cultural barriers. We note that the field of ethnomusicology increasingly advocates for performance as an approach "for research outcomes that are sited in original performative know-ledge, explored, produced and delivered through performance itself" (McKerrell, 2022, pp. 10–11). We agree, yet also recognize enormous potential for this to occur through a productive fusion with artistic research developed through the use of "stimulated recall," as encapsulated in the shared listenings demonstrated throughout this publication.

In the remainder of Section 1, we will set the stage by exploring the notion of decolonized listening, followed by discussion of musical subjectivities as a performance quality, and their extension to second- and third-person perspectives, and of issues for technologies in the mediation of musical sound and image. In Section 2 we describe the background of knowledge and previous studies in which our work is situated, including the latest theories and research findings concerning musical memory and cognition, the evolution of audiovisual technologies in research generally and music research in particular, and both how and why video-based stimulated recall methods came to be applied in

---

[6] Artistic research was implemented in most European countries in the early 2000s. The term is less common in the UK, where practice-as-research is a rather synonymous approach (Nelson, 2022). However, the term has also gained currency in the UK, as can be seen in recent publications such as Blain and Minors (2020). However, in most countries, there is a prehistory of gradual development of formats for artistic research in conservatories, dating back to the 1970s. In Finland, doctoral degrees were awarded in academies of fine and performing arts already in the late 1980s. For further reading see Biggs and Karlsson (2011) and Östersjö, Stefan. (2019).

innovative ways throughout our project. Section 3 chronicles how specific musical insights and discoveries were made through the coding and re-coding of interactions through the ensemble's shared listenings approach to stimulated recall methods. Section 4 depicts how, through the Musical Transformations project, the ensemble's approach was applied within a project in Vietnam in cooperation with traditional music performers. The publication ends with Section 5, in which we synthesize the main concepts and offer a summary discussion of our findings and the implications of a shared listenings approach for intercultural ensemble development in other settings, particularly higher education institutions. Note that the structure of this Element is intentionally concise, which inevitably entails a number of delimitations. There will be very few opportunities here to offer any analysis of the characteristics of Vietnamese music culture, contemporary experimental Western art music, sociohistorical contexts, or ethnomusicological theory, but rather our focus is deliberately practical: how transcultural music projects can be more equitably pursued and meaningfully studied through decolonized approaches to intercultural collaboration.

Decolonizing Listening

In November 2019, music theorist Philip Ewell delivered a keynote presentation at the Society for Music Theory (SMT), which described the "whiteness" of music theory through Fegin's concept of "the white racial frame" (2009). Ewell argued that Fegin's "frame" illuminates the structural framework through which music theory, like other academic fields, has continued to "privilege the compositional and theoretical work of whites over non-whites" (Ewell, 2021, n.p.). Drawing also on Sara Ahmed's critique of the discourse of diversity (2012), Ewell pointed to how change cannot be merely a matter of cosmetic changes with reference to inclusion. Ewell, an African American scholar, has also drawn attention to the role of the white racial frame as a structural source for inequity in various publications,[7] and it seems increasingly clear that music theory may be entering a new paradigm through reflection on these concerns. In essence, the present-day search within academic institutions for decolonizing principles for

---

[7] In a recent paper, Ewell develops the same argument that one of the foundation stones of musicology, Schenkerian analysis, is based on a framework built on outspoken racism (Ewell, 2020). Ewell observes how the hierarchical structure of Schenkerian analysis, which builds on the assumption that the background layer, the *ursatz*, must govern the middle ground and foreground. He further argues that there is an immediate relation between the foundations of Schenkerian music theory and his explicit racism, implying "that blacks are inferior because only the white German genius, with superior *Menschenhumus*, is capable of producing the background that Schenker speaks of" (Ewell, 2020, n.p.). Ewell's keynote presentation sparked an agitated response from music theorists and, in particular, Schenker analysis scholars. Clearly, the

curriculum renewal rests on an unprecedented willingness to "question the epistemological authority assigned uniquely to the Western university as the privileged site of knowledge production" (Bhambra, Gebrial, & Nişancıoğlu, 2018, p. 3). This entails a systematic exposure of the "material, intellectual and symbolic colonialism that abounds in the university system" (Saini & Begum, 2020, p. 218). Hence, the aim of decolonization points beyond the strife for diversity, toward a fundamental reconsideration, and a widening of the foundations of knowledge within academia. This also implies that in music research, not only do theory and methods need to be decolonized but also the very foundations of our embodied practices, including our *listening*. In his recent book, *Hungry Listening: Resonant Theory for Indigenous Sound Studies (Indigenous Americas)* (2020), Dylan Robinson also addressed the problem of racism in musical listening. One way he accomplished this was by quoting one of the most celebrated sound artists and composers, R. Murray Schafer, who laid the ground for the world soundscape project and who famously theorized listening as a vehicle for an ecological understanding of the relation between human and environment. Robinson opened his book on the ethical foundations of intercultural communication with how Schafer found that the "eskimos are such an astonishingly unmusical race that the composer really has to wring his material to make it musically presentable" (Schafer 1961, cited in Robinson, 2020, p. 8). It is indeed an astonishing statement, compressing into a few words a multitude of prejudices that have been integral to much intercultural music practice, in which composers have appropriated indigenous music for their own purposes and, as Ewell would describe it, listened to their music through a white racial frame. Indeed, our listening "is guided by positionality as an intersection of perceptual habit, ability and bias" (Robinson 2020, p. 45), and Schafer's statement is expressive of how a listening *habitus* (Becker, 2010) can deprive us of the ability to truly listen to a musical Other (Östersjö, 2020). Robinson (2020) observes how Schafer's "words sonify compositional violence" (p. 8) and, to the contrary, proposes a decolonized "critical listening positionality," which would "prompt questions regarding how we might become better attuned to the particular filters of race, class, gender and ability that actively select and frame the moment of contact between listening body and listened-to sound" (p. 11). The challenge of decolonization concerns art worlds and science worlds alike, but the extent to which it entails the performative transformation of embodied practices is perhaps most clearly seen within the arts. How can we bend our ears

---

response, which filled almost the entire twelfth issue of the *Journal of Schenkerian Studies* (2019) illustrated that the issues addressed by Ewell are indeed profound. However, Schenkerian theory serves only as an example here. There is a need for decolonizing theory and methods in academia across disciplines.

to listen beyond the "white racial frame" described by Ewell? How can we approach musical Others through an approach to listening that evades the compositional violence of colonialism?

Some of the earliest calls for decolonization of research methods are from 1999 in the seminal writings of Maori scholar Linda Tuhiwai Smith (2012) who, among other things, pointed to how the systems of knowledge that developed with the Enlightenment and continued through modernity:

> [N]ot only informed the field of study referred to by Said as "Orientalism" but other disciplines of knowledge and "regimes of truth." It is through these disciplines that the Indigenous world has been represented to the West and it is through these disciplines that Indigenous peoples often research for the fragments of ourselves which were taken, catalogued, studied and stored. (Smith, 2012, p. 67)

Decolonization has recently become a topic across many academic fields (Connell, 2018; Mbembe, 2016). The global movement to "decolonize" universities and academic subjects is rooted in legitimate concerns associated with the inadequacies of a Eurocentric orientation (Hebert, 2023), which is caused by an incomplete scientific project traceable to colonial antecedents (Richardson, 2018). Anthropologists and other scholars associated with the decolonizing movement have aimed to bring recognition to the historical bases for academic disciplines that were "founded in relation to dominant imperial and white supremacist logics" and they have "put forward a platform of decolonial anthropological practice, pedagogy, and public engagement" (Thomas, 2018, p. 393). Anthropology has especially seen painful introspection on the field's colonial history (Allen & Jobson, 2016), and during efforts to "decolonize" the anthropology curriculum at the University of Cambridge, the staff acknowledged "the 'uncomfortable' relationship between anthropologists as intellectual producers at the 'cutting edge' of the canon, and the discipline's rife colonial residues" (Mogstad & Tse, 2018).

As the first academic field to emphasize cross-cultural research, anthropology has often deeply influenced ethnomusicology in terms of both theories and methods, about which Liz Mackinlay has questioned: "What kind of discipline is ethnomusicology with/out decolonizing talk, and further, is talk alone enough to decolonize?" (2015, p. 8). Ethnomusicology – the global study of music in human life – now evidently seeks to identify effective ways of improving its diversity and openness as a field. In their "Open Letter from SEM Past Presidents on Racism" (SEM 2020), ten former presidents of the Society for Ethnomusicology (SEM) recently acknowledged that "[d]eep-seated white supremacy and colonialism shape SEM, and SEM is a site in which these systems of power are produced and reproduced. This situation demands a strong and proactive response." This public admission came even while some noted with caution that such discussions can become hypercritical and even risk "degenerating into unhelpful binaries of Culture Wars-led identity politics" (Tan, 2021, p. 5; see also Moosavi, 2020).

Earlier publications have asserted that "[d]ecolonizing methodologies, as an approach, is especially relevant to ethnomusicologists from indigenous backgrounds with an interest in studying the history of their own people's music" (Hebert & McCollum 2014, p. 134). Still, although there are "unique advantages to indigenous scholarship that emphasizes a decidedly introspective orientation" (Hebert & McCollum, 2014, p. 12), we suggest here that a decolonized approach can be relevant to all musicians and music scholars. Chávez and Skelchy (2019) argue that "the impulse to theorize in ethnomusicology has contributed to the abstraction of decolonization from practical applications" (p. 116), and as a more concrete way of *decolonizing ethnomusicology*, they support "collaboration between ethnomusicologists, composers, and musicologists, which can take the form of publications, musical compositions, or live performance. The benefit of these collaborations could be furthering a dialogue about decolonization in music departments that addresses ways of listening, composing, and thinking about music studies" (p. 138). It is in such a way that decolonial approaches may be especially relevant to intercultural music ensembles.

In the field of live performance there are also ongoing discussions concerning colonialism and how it is a part of a power structure that defines boundaries between categories of music. In a recent article, musician and scholar George Lewis (2021) concludes that "I feel that we already know what colonialism sounds like. We hear it at all too many contemporary music festivals around the world" (para. 2). Lewis further argues, however, that "the composers and improvisers are not the ones producing the sounds of colonialism" (para. 2), but it is rather the politics of cultural institutions and curators that enforce a colonial structure. This is an experience that is shared by The Six Tones and perhaps related to the liberating change of the group's identity toward becoming active on the experimental music scene in Vietnam rather than only as a player on the European scene, a point we will come back to in Section 3. Deliberate efforts to escape a scene that had long been shaped by colonial attitudes paved the way for developing new understandings of our shared musical work.

When the ensemble engages with traditional Vietnamese culture, it is from the perspective of intercultural collaboration, and thereby it could be argued that the group seeks to understand and explore the artistic potentiality in transculturation. Transculturation, seen as "a long-term, polyphonic, and multi-sited social process and complex dynamic" (Koch, 2021), can be, in a sense, the opposite of decolonization. However, even if transculturation denotes processes of hybridization, and decolonization may be understood as the acknowledgment of systems of thought – as well as practices other than those of colonial and Eurocentric origin – we have also seen how they come together in the inter-cultural and collaborative practice of the group. Related is the more general ambition of musical change of the Eurocentric new music milieu in the West. Returning to Lewis, there is a corresponding need to

> invent a new, incarnative "we" that understands contemporary music not as a globalized, pan-European, white sonic diaspora, but more like the blues, practiced by the widest variety of people in many variations around the world. If this new "we" can embrace "our" future, even with all its turbulence, if we can place ourselves conceptually in the situation of a creole, we can reaffirm our common humanity in the pursuit of new music decolonization. (Lewis, 2021)

Listening and Subjectivity

To better understand the ways in which musical expression is communicated between performing musicians in real time, it is also necessary to understand the processes and attributes that shape these expressions. Since 2006, The Six Tones has been trying to unravel how some of those processes interact and are influenced by the cultural contexts that the respective members bring to the group. From the very beginning the ensemble consciously tried to understand both the intra- and extra-musical aspects of our communications by studying our own interactions in the group, as well as those with other musicians. This is by no means easy to do even with a good method at hand, and it is a practice that raises social and political questions that are as important as they are complex.

Musical practice in group performance is a communicative interaction between at least three modalities: communicating individuality, adapting to the current context, and relating to the musical and cultural practice of each of the participating musicians. Though this model is a crude reduction of some-thing as volatile and difficult to grasp as musical interaction and performance, it nonetheless serves the purpose of conceptualizing some of the necessary con-ditions for inter-cultural musical practice. The primary purpose here is to show how and why The Six Tones has worked with the methods described in this publication and why a decolonized perspective has been necessary.

Similar to gender, "musical identity is performed – we inscribe upon our-selves an emergent musical subjectivity through acts of performance and perception" (Stover, 2016, n.p.). This may also be referred to as the musician's individual voice (Cumming, 2000; Gorton & Östersjö, 2019). As proposed by Gorton and Östersjö – expanding Cone's (1974) and Cumming's (2000) conceptions of voice in musical performance by combining a perspective drawn from embodied cognition with Bourdieu's sociological concept of habitus – "interactions between performers and their instruments are combined with other interactions in the formation of a performer's 'voice': with composers, with musical scores, and with the contextual practices within which the performer operates" (2019, p. 44). However, theories of embodiment must be understood through Fanon's critique of Merlau-Ponty's notion "that there is a normative pre-personal corporeal schema that all humans share and it is this corporeal schema as a biological given that cannot be fundamentally altered by society, culture and language" (Mahendran, 2007, p. 198). Hence, subjectivity as an emergent quality in musical performance can only be fully understood through an analysis of the sociocultural context in which it is situated. If the subjectivity of a musician constitutes one modality, the sociocultural context can be divided in two further modalities, situation and tradition. The situation entails the current context for the playing, including the acoustics of the room, any listeners present, and also what kind of performative activity this is, for example, if it is a rehearsal, a concert, or a situation not covered by these two. The tradition, finally, is a musical and cultural context that partakes in shaping the habitus of each participating musician.

The subjective stance of each musician is continuously negotiated and shaped by the context and the musical framework of all other participating musicians. In most classical music ensembles, a musical and cultural tradition is tacitly shared by all musicians and contributes to the encapsulation of the interpretative framework. For instance, in a string quartet playing common-practice European art music from the Romantic era, a shared knowledge between the four musicians shapes the communication across these modalities. This knowledge is an essential part of the performance tradition connected to the style of music being performed.

Intercultural collaboration immediately problematizes the dynamic of these relations. In the case of The Six Tones, we did not initially possess such a common cultural context, nor did we even have a shared knowledge of the musical traditions of all members in the group. Not even for relatively basic concepts, such as *improvisation*, was a common understanding shared across the group. Hence, it was necessary to approach rehearsals and performances taking these facts into account. An additional factor we had to systematically confront and negotiate was that in a number of different ways – social privilege, academic standing, cultural insider status, linguistic competence, economic resources, and so on – power relations in the group were not equally distributed.

It is not possible to immediately embody and understand any culture different from one's own, and a search for listening beyond the "white racial frame" is a challenge that demands both time and effort. While there are indeed moments in which musicians learn almost instantaneously from one another, as a general rule it may take weeks, months, or even many years to fully embody performance techniques and musical styles, as will be demonstrated in Section 3. For The Six Tones, the realization that mutual learning was not a feasible method for intercultural collaboration led to the joint finding of a different way of conceptualizing their work. Here, Glissant's notion of the right to opacity, and the related concept of coexistence, became a different model. As the group began to explore this approach, the need for new forms of listening became apparent. What this research seeks to explore is how the process of decolonizing the listening practices of the group has been aided by the method of stimulated recall.

Learning through all three of the modalities mentioned already is common practice for most competent musicians, whether or not one consciously reflects upon it. Interdisciplinary and intercultural collaborations, however, may be far more complex. As mentioned earlier, the challenges tend to not be evenly distributed across the members of the ensemble, and each challenge comes with a complex history and traditions. Deliberately questioning the frame and decolonizing our practice clearly engender sometimes uncomfortable destabilization in the group dynamic, but this is an often necessary step toward an altered musical practice.

The disruptive effect that new knowledge can have on performance practice may eventually pave the way for new possibilities, new expressions, and yet new modes of listening. The goal of such decolonized systems of musical thinking is not to create a new standard or singular scheme of inter-operations but rather to point to a multiplicity of possibilities. As Foucault indicates, using phrasing that inadvertently applies well to music,

> it is by no means a matter of determining *the* system of thought of a particular epoch, or something like its "world-view." Rather, it is a matter of identifying the different ensembles that are each bearers of a quite particular type of knowledge; that connect behaviors, rules of conduct, laws, habits, or prescriptions; that thus form configurations both stable and capable of transformation. Is also a matter of defining relations of conflict, proximity or exchange. Systems of thought are forms in which, during a given period of time, the knowledges individualize, achieve an equilibrium, and enter into communication. (Foucault 1997, p. 9)

Following this it is through a composition of systems of thought that decolonization of the habits, knowledges, and past experiences becomes possible, and where knowledge is both disembodied and embodied, thus making knowledge communicable. Elsewhere Foucault describes a method for a "progressive exercise of memorization" (p. 101): (1) the importance of listening, (2) the importance of writing, and (3) the importance of self-reflection. That these three points map well onto the practice of music will be shown later in this text, but for now it is essential to point out that to *listen to the other* is often recognized as a central aspect of *ethics* (Cobussen & Nielsen, 2012; Frisk, 2014; Nguyễn & Östersjö, 2019). The particular characteristic of the listening that Foucault referred to here is both active and contemplative, and respectful toward what is heard. Writing, in the context of the practice of The Six Tones, could be understood as the generative phase allowing for a re-actualization of experiences. This could be enacted through the sedimentation of embodied knowledge in performance or by way of making audio recordings. Finally, self-reflection is the activity of searching within oneself by rereading from memory and understanding the hidden values of acquired knowledge.

As will be shown in Section 4, similar processes that represent these three stages are further explored through the use of novel stimulated recall methods that The Six Tones developed. It is a way in which we have been allowed to initiate complex exercises of subject formation, analysis, and intersubjective learning. In short, it is a process in which the members of the group are allowed to reflect on the activities through which the music is created. These activities may also be traced to cultural, social, or even political aspects of the roles each musician occupies, the main purpose of which has been to decolonize the development of the ensemble's music as well as the knowledge produced within the group. The objective was to encourage discourses and narratives that make it possible to approach everything from the tiniest musical materials to the overall shape or form of the performances and to process new knowledge. At best, this allows the artistic process to be more even, power structures less prominent, and relations more equal.

The actual status of subjectivity and the idea of a fixed identity as an inner essence that shapes actions and possibilities in the world has been questioned many times (Frisk, 2013), but the interaction between a subject and the knowledge it possesses vis-à-vis the contexts in which it operates is an important factor in all ensemble practices. Such an identity may first be seen to be at odds with a common view of the artist's subjective self, key to the highly valued *personality* of the contemporary musician whose inner core is the stability of their expressive power. But through analyses of intercultural collaboration, in this publication we argue that the subjectivity of a decolonized musician is constantly negotiated through listening (knowledge), writing (embodying), and self-reflection (restructuring).

This process is referred to by Foucault (1997) as the *techniques of the self*, which may allow for rethinking subjectively organized and acquired power, and he specifically posed the question, "How should one 'govern oneself' by performing actions in which one is oneself the objective of those actions, the domain in which they are brought to bear, the instrument they employ, and the subject that acts?" (p. 87).

These techniques of the self are somewhat related to the process discussed in this publication through the work of The Six Tones: a process of devising a decolonized method that allows us to ask similar questions in intercultural collaborations, from a uniquely musical point of view. As we will demonstrate, this is through a continuous process of disrupting the power of the imperative of the known self and reconfiguring both listening and subjectivity in a fluid interaction between the various agents in the collaboration, as well as the performance's cultural context and the musical and cultural backgrounds of the musicians.

Second-Person Perspective

The reflection on subjectivity and power relations given earlier, and the methods used to recognize and counteract their negative impact, not only develops self-awareness but also points to the complexity between the role of subjectivity in relation to the formation of intersubjectivity. The notion of "the other" and the aspect of ethics in the meeting with "the other" have been thoroughly explored and discussed by the French philosopher Emmanuel Levinas. His claim that the relationship with the Other precedes all ontology (Levinas, 1979, p. 48) as a *first philosophy* clearly gives intersubjectivity a particular status.

In musical performances there are at least two somewhat distinct articulations of intersubjectivity: the first is the actual meeting of the other; the second, of particular interest in this discussion, is the meeting mediated by playing music. While it is difficult to claim that the latter does not rest on ontology, it still shares some of the aspects of the first one, the face-to-face meeting. In this case music acts as a proxy in the intersubjectivity but nevertheless one that is closely entangled with both the performer and the other musician(s). Musical interaction, from this ethical perspective between individuals in music-making, is conceptualized by Rahaim (2017) as a metaphysics of unity and alterity. These relations are built on an intention to approach the Other – an acceptance and "absorption of the Other into an overarching unity" (Rahaim, 2017, p. 223). In music performance the unity is mediated through sound and may embody "a dialogical relation between culturally distinct others" (Östersjö & Nguyễn, 2019, p. 286). Along the same lines, Cobussen and Nielsen (2012) further claim that "a musical ethics can only come into existence on the basis of a contact with a perceiver – that is, through the act of listening. Thus, ethical moments can only be understood as strategies of engagement, through receptive interpretation, affected and formed by both doubt and astonishment" (2012, p. 166).

That "the particularity of the self can get in the way" (Frisk, 2013) in meetings with the other, also in music, is obvious. In intercultural interactions, inconsiderate actions may easily mask significant or rare aspects of some of the musical expressions explored (Emmerson, 2006). This may be the result of some system of domination or unequal relationship that has not yet been properly addressed, and any such imbalance needs to be brought to the fore, but it can also be the result of merely a lack of knowledge of the other. But even then there are risks related to what Žižek calls "liberal multiculturalism as an experience of Other deprived of its Otherness" (Žižek, 2011). In other words, the question is how intersubjectivity can be developed in an intercultural setting while allowing difference to be an asset and Otherness be a rich quality that allows performers equal opportunities and capacity for action.

The complexity of the emic/etic perspectives of ethnographic research embodies the need for decolonized methods in which the knowledge construction emerges primarily from musicians inside a specific musical tradition (Agawu, 2003; Hebert & McCollum, 2014; Smith, 2012; Solomon, 2012). But, as pointed out by Smith (2012), the emic/etic perspective is a core challenge, which must be addressed in the development of decolonized methods:

> Indigenous research approaches problematize the insider model in different ways because there are multiple ways of both being an insider and an outsider in indigenous contexts. The critical issue with insider research is the constant need for reflexivity. At a general level insider researchers have to have ways of thinking critically about their processes, their relationships and the quality and richness of their data and analysis. (Smith, 2012, p. 137)

From the very beginning, the aim of The Six Tones was to create music with an identity that was neither Vietnamese, nor Swedish, nor European, but a music with its own distinct character. We wanted to avoid the simple superimposition of one tradition on top of the other, instead aiming for the coexistence of the two elements on equal grounds, far from the politically driven idea of multicultural expressions. The idea of intersubjectivity is at the heart of this ambition. It is possible to develop the idea through new models of cognitive science as presented by Gallese (2014) building on a second-person perspective:

"The second-person perspective offers a different and deflationary epistemic approach to the problem of other minds, by reducing the mental gap that supposedly separates them" (p. 2). If Levinas's interpretation of the meeting with the other, structured by sensitivity, takes place pre-cognitively, the subconscious and conscious part of the encounter is concerned with reflections upon the other, objectifying, perceiving, and predicting them through a third-person perspective. But, as pointed out by Gallese (2014),

> we do not only mentally entertain an "objective" third-person account of what others are, do to us and with us. When relating to others, we also experience them as bodily selves, similar to how we experience ourselves as the owners of our body and the authors of our actions. When exposed to others' expressive behaviours, reactions and inclinations, we simultaneously experience their goal-directedness intentional character, as we experience ourselves as the agents of our actions, the subjects of our affects, feelings and emotions, the owners of our thoughts, fantasies, imaginations and dreams. All of these peculiar qualities of our social transactions qualify as ingredients of the so-called second-person perspective on intersubjectivity. (p. 5)

Centering of intersubjectivity as a middle ground between the subjective and dominant agency of the "I" and the distanced reflection and objectification that the third-person perspective gives has been a driving force in the development of the methods discussed in this publication and also in the artistic development of the ensemble.

Self-reflection through stimulated recall can be challenging due to the inherent contradictions of simultaneously seeking intersubjectivity while also reflecting on one's own perceptions and behaviors as an agent within the performance context. Moreover, this is also partly because reflection is in itself a problematic concept, as it often fails to adequately depict what it actually constitutes. Reflection may even be casually regarded as part of everything one does, at all times. Furthermore, as Catherine Laws (2019) points out, "[a]s soon as an individual attempts to speak from a particular moment or situation – to speak subjectively of the subjective experience – she turns herself into an object" (p. 17). At that point one is no longer part of the action, "distanced from the dynamics of the subject position and no longer able to speak through it" (p. 19).

In order to explicate the role of subjectivity and relationality in research methods, Liora Bresler (2009) turns to existential philosopher Martin Buber's conceptualization of connections between objectivity and detachment on the one hand and the need for creating "responsive, improvised procedures, based on the recognition of interactions and the dynamic nature of what we study" (p. 11) on the other. Cobussen and Nielsen (2012) remind us that, in music research, the act of listening is also an ethical moment, which builds on engagement with the Other and is "affected and formed by both doubt and astonishment" (p. 166). Bresler proposes that detachment is a complementary aspect of responsivity, leading to the notion that "detachment from habitual and practical forms of seeing" can initiate a process of making the familiar strange, thereby going "beyond decoding and recognition towards heightened perception" (p. 12). Reflective consideration of internal processes of this kind is essential in order to gain a deep understanding of each individual's "inner world" as a basis for the complex relationships associated with intercultural collaboration in ensemble music creation. To this end, the essence of individual experience must be captured to the fullest extent possible, which is why phenomenological considerations also play an important role in this research.

Moreover, stimulated recall methods are deeply entwined with the audio and video technologies on which its procedures rest, so with the aim of considering the agency of these technologies, we now turn to discussion of a phenomenological perspective.

Listening and Mediation

In music research, important milestones in the use of phenomenological methods are Pierre Schaeffer's classic study *Treatise on Musical Objects: An Essay across Disciplines* (2017/1966) and, in more recent years, Jonathan De Souza's *Music at Hand* (2017). What both of these projects propose is that phenomenology offers methods for approaching the lived experience of music and sound, such as methods for phenomenological reduction, developed by Schaeffer, and of phenomenological variation as found in the work of De Souza (following Husserl and Ihde). As a central expression of Eurocentric thinking, phenomenology may not easily be combined with a decolonized perspective. Frantz Fanon reminds us that "what is given to description is never simply given; it is in large part imposed through the culture" (Bernasconi, 2020, p. 406), as we have already observed earlier. Hence, in our understanding, it is necessary to approach phenomenological practices through a critical, and decolonized, perspective, "opening the path to a phenomenology dedicated to disalienation or, we might say today, decolonization, in which the norms of Whiteness are challenged" (Bernasconi, 2020, p. 406).

Phenomenology has constituted a varied framework in several artistic research projects. For Arlander (2008) it was the impetus for creative work, while in other projects, phenomenology has been a means for the analysis of artistic outputs (Unander-Scharin, 2008) or a way to share new insights into sensory experience and bodily experience of touch (Elo & Luoto, 2018).

In music research, stimulated recall rests on a "robust foundation in listening and its engagement with the sonic representation and documentation of artistic process and artefacts" (Östersjö, 2020, p. 95). The invention of the tape recorder was a precondition, a technology the usage of which is perhaps best understood through Schaeffer's early observations of how a group of listeners would not make the same description of the same sound object. Even though the tape recorder was able to play back the exact same physical signal, each listener always approaches a sound object from a certain predisposition (Schaeffer, 2017). This may be understood as involving different intentionalities, and the difference between human and techno-logical intentionality is here described by Ihde (2007):

> I go to the auditorium, and, without apparent effort, I hear the speaker while I barely notice the scuffling of feet, the coughing, the scraping noises. My tape recorder, not having the same intentionality as I, records all these auditory stimuli without distinction, and so when I return to it to hear the speech re-presented I find I cannot even hear the words due to the presence of what for me had been fringe phenomena. The tape recorder's "sense data" intentionality has changed the phenomenon. (Ihde, 2007, p. 75)

Verbeek (2008) observes how there is a "double intentionality involved here; one of technology toward 'its' world, and one of human beings toward the result of this technological intentionality" (p. 393). While technology to some extent is directed toward representing phenomena in the world, others are rather directed toward constructing realities. The relation between human and techno-logical intentionality, Verbeek analyzes as a "composite intentionality," which is "directed at making accessible ways in which technologies 'experience' the world" (Verbeek, 2008, p. 393).

However, human intentionality is always related to the temporal nature of lived experience, and when an auditory stimulus is repeatedly played back in a stimulated recall situation (see Figure 1), each instance takes place as a separate lived experience (L_{0-3}). In the figure we see a graphical representation of a stimulated recall process, analyzed from the perspective of composite intentionality. Human intentionality is influenced by the possibilities afforded by technological intentionality, resulting in an enhanced understanding of the original situation that goes beyond the scope of mere recollection. The reflections on previous lived experiences are combinations of different constellations of earlier lived experiences allowing for both reflections and meta-reflections. The image is a modification of an illustration by Vermersch (1999), to which we have added the perspective of technological intentionality. Repetitions of stimulated recall are plotted on the *x*-axis allowing for a continual phenomenological reduction (*y*-axis).

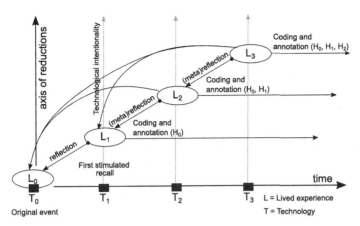

Figure 1 A representation of experience and technology-stimulated reflections building on Vermersch (1999)

Schaeffer's discovery of acousmatic listening built on observations of how the tape recorder's ability to further parse a recording into perceptual units or sound objects also offered new possibilities for research in music. For Schaeffer (2017), the tape recorder was "first and foremost (for research purposes), a machine for observing sounds, for 'decontextualizing' them, for rediscovering traditional objects, listening again to traditional music with a different ear, an ear that, if not new, is at least as deconditioned as possible" (p. 16). A fundamental principle of stimulated recall is the instruction for the observer to stop the playback at any moment, which attracts attention. In music research using stimulated recall, this method effectively becomes a parallel to the analysis of sound on an object level proposed by Schaeffer and builds on the earlier-mentioned composite intentionality of human and technology.

In stimulated recall, there are several modes of perception involved: outward, listening to one's own or others' sounds, mediated through the technology, and inward, listening to past experiences and memory representations. Both of these modes continuously coexist and interact with one another (Frisk & Karlsson, 2010). Further, a subject (re-)experiences thought processes that are layered in time and space and encompass both analytical and musical thinking.

2 Technology-Driven Advancements in Performance Studies

Introduction

Music is a profoundly meaningful human activity that is nonetheless notoriously difficult to describe. Across history, scholars have endeavored to produce rich descriptions of music using various approaches, from subjective and often metaphorical claims about its impact on people to the use of notation systems to transcribe and analyze its components and forms. In this section we will consider the current state of research in multiple fields connected with how newer technologies increasingly enhance our ability to understand music, as well as to make sense of *musical understanding* itself. This is particularly seen in video-based "stimulated recall" studies that enable rich exploration of how musicians retrospectively interpret their behaviors. The latter half of this section traces the introduction of these approaches into research and how the methods have been adopted in music studies.

Audio and Video Recordings in Music Research

The development and popularization of *sound* recordings from the late nineteenth century onward was a revolution unlike any other in music history, creating unprecedented possibilities for both the experience of music and our understanding of music itself. In this section we aim to argue that the same is true – albeit to a somewhat lesser degree and for different purposes – for the popularization of *video* recording technology of musical performances, but it has taken many years for scholars to fully recognize the unique potential of video as a tool supporting music research and artistic development.

Access to video recording technology evolved across decades, as video surpassed film as a technology that would become affordable to the general population and was ultimately built into common smartphones. By the 1980s video technologies had become sufficiently accessible via tech labs at universities that researchers began to examine how its application might bring entirely new insights into various fields. By the 1990s video was an essential tool in many natural sciences, but its adoption was slower in most social sciences. Research using such approaches began with film, a relatively expensive and less-accessible technology, but later it was eclipsed by video. Stanford University's Center for Advanced Study in the Behavioral Sciences has been credited with pioneering the "first systematic attempt at simultaneous analysis of verbal and nonverbal aspects of social interaction" in 1955–6 with a team led by psychologist Frieda Fromm-Reichman, which included notable anthropologist Gregory Bateson, among others (Erickson, 2011, p. 180). By the 1970s video was starting to be used by some social scientists, but it remained a rather expensive and cumbersome technology for many years.

The notion of stimulated recall may be traced to Benjamin Bloom – the American educational psychologist renowned for "Bloom's Taxonomy" – who reflected on the educational potential of film and television and observed that "underlying the method of stimulated recall is that a subject may be enabled to relive an original situation with vividness and accuracy if he is presented with a large number of the cues or stimuli which occurred during the original situation" (Bloom, 1953, p. 161). While Bloom could not easily have predicted in 1953 the possibilities that would later be enabled by video technology, these aims are exactly what video would later support in research of this kind. With regard to the use of video, the work of Kagan and colleagues (Kagan & Krathwohl, 1967) was important. They developed the method further by – rather than using selected clips, as in Bloom's study – asking each subject to view the entire documentation and to stop it to identify moments that required comment. In terms of theoretical contributions, other notable figures in this field have been Australian semiotician Gunther Kress (1940–2019), who collaborated with Dutch linguist (and jazz pianist) Theo van Leeuwen (b.1947) in development of the field of social semiotics and the notion of *multimodality* (Kress & van Leeuwen, 2001).

In the 1980s the method attracted researchers in music psychology and music pedagogy. Marlene Taylor's study from 1985 is focused on children's experiences of music listening. She uses video-stimulated recall as one of several methods as a "means of probing into the thought structures of the child's world" (Taylor, 1985, p. 32). In the final discussion she notes how, in the interviews,

> [i]t is not clear whether or not a child is recalling the original thought or if, indeed, it is possible to recall a thought in its original state. The act of reflection and its effect on the recall of thought is not known; however, it does appear that these children recall some of their thoughts and can comment upon them. (p. 36)

Taylor's observations remain pertinent, although we find, with reference to the discussion of composite intentionality in the previous section, that the stimulated recall situation may be better understood as reflection and metareflection, rather than "recalling" an earlier experience, since each reflection may be better understood as a new lived experience.

Toward an Oral History of the Field

As part of developing the present Element we determined that rather than merely offering a formal literature review and description of methodology it would be especially valuable to interview the researchers whom we regard as pioneers in this field. As we approached researchers for interviews, we explained that we sought their reflections regarding the inspiration, opportunities, and challenges associated with this kind of approach to examining musical topics and that we hoped to collect information from our predecessors who had developed original work in this area as a way of establishing a clearer sense of the origins, innovations, and future prospects for video-based stimulated recall as a multimodal method in music research. Additionally, we explained that although we seek to demonstrate a particular method of video-stimulated recall among musicians, we also want to give credit where credit is due for the intellectual lineage of this approach.

Bastien and Hostager

Early pioneers of video-based methods for music research from the field of communications include David T. Bastien and Todd J. Hostager, who collaborated on a series of articles from the late 1980s that featured examination of videos as a method for analysis of communication among jazz musicians in the course of live performance (Bastien & Hostager, 1988, 1992, 1996). The researchers are based in the Midwestern United States, where David Bastien has recently worked as an adjunct professor of communication at St. Cloud State University (Minnesota) and as a private consultant for business mergers and acquisitions, while Todd J. Hostager has served as a director of Digital Strategy Curriculum for Logic PD after retiring as a professor of management at the University of Wisconsin–Eau Claire.

From our interviews, we discovered that David Bastien came from an unusually musical family and that Todd Hostager was a fellow doctoral student with whom he collaborated in the music research that was partly inspired by jazz bands that included Bastien's father:

> My grandfather ran a town band in a mining town of Minnesota, and had eight children, all of whom were great musicians, six of whom became fairly successful professional musicians. My late father was Gene Krupa's bassist from '39 through '41. After he was released from the army in 1946, he moved back to the Twin Cities where he was the "go to" bassist for traveling jazz acts and pops concerts. He was a full-time member of the WCCO AM radio band until 1958. He also was the "go to" bassist for Orchestra Hall's pops concerts and many other shows. My cousin Jim Hughart was hired by Ella Fitzgerald upon his release from the army in 1959 or so. He can also be heard on Tom Waits' early albums. He was with Natalie Cole for the whole multi-year run of her "Unforgettable" show. (Bastien, 2022).

Bastien especially credits sociologist Carl Couch (Chen, 1995) for inspiring some of his work, based on the perspective of symbolic interactionism: "I was seriously influenced by Carl Couch at University of Iowa" (Bastien, 2022). According to Bastien, Carl Couch was especially seeking to understand how people respond to emergency situations in the 1970s and 1980s and had noted how video was a uniquely useful tool. Bastien surmised that video would also be a helpful way of understanding better how jazz musicians interact through improvisation within a set of rules on a basic musical structure: "I have believed all along that videorecording represents a coming wave of reality and that researchers in sociology, communication, and social psychology have not caught up with it yet. Carl was the first person I could find who was doing that kind of research" (Bastien, 2022).

Bastien described how this early video-based music research collaboration began as follows:

> My Dad did a concert around '88 and I was back at the graduate school talking with my dissertation advisor Andrew H. Van de Ven and a colleague. They kept asking questions about jazz that made it obvious to me they didn't get how it was done. I explained, "You've got to know the chords, you've got to know the harmonic structure, and once you know that, you can figure it out." (Bastien, 2022)

One of the most curious was Todd Hostager, one of Bastien's fellow graduate students, who lacked the intimate familiarity with such music that Bastien had obtained through his own family. As Bastien explains, Hostager kept asking "how can these people do this? It's magic." Luckily, it turned out that the concert had been videotaped commercially.

> I was able to get a hold of the producer of the concert, a PhD from the University of Iowa. I wanted to be able to explain how musicians who are ordinary folk can do this, since people who are not from that musical environment think it is magic, that God just gave them all this stuff. (Bastien, 2022)

Later, "Todd and I went through the entire tape, stopping every instant" (Bastien, 2022). In this way, despite primarily being scholars of business communications, Bastian and Hostager also became some of the earliest researchers to explore video's potential for analysis of interactions among musicians (Bastien & Hostager, 1988, 1992, 1996). These studies enabled them to explain that in business and other fields there is much to learn from the lesson of human interactions seen within improvisational practices in music. Bastien summarized these insights in the following way:

> In one of our 1988 publications, we said that what people need to improvise are the same insights as to the theory of the task being done. All productive human social activity is governed by a kind of knowledge and rules. There is a theory, for instance, if you go into an operating room or any other context, people who are strangers can cooperate with each other because they all understand what the task is in fundamentally the same terms. (Bastien, 2022)

Ultimately, Bastien and Hostager reached the conclusion that "[a]ll human tasks are fundamentally organized the same way jazz is. That you have a fundamental structure around which you build everything, and people have to act within that structure according to the needs the structure presents to them" (Bastien, 2022). Indeed, the collaboration between Bastien and Hostager demonstrated that video-based examination of musician interactions can offer broader insights into how deep human cooperation can lead to great achievements, and soon other researchers would continue in further development of studies of this kind.

Kempe and West

Scandinavia has also been an important early source of pioneering studies in the field of video analysis of musical practices. Since 2001, a collaboration between Anna-Lena Kempe (née Rostvall) and Tore West has produced several publications that use video for analysis of interactions between musicians. The outcomes have included not only articles in music journals and proceedings but also articles concerning their innovative methodology itself in such journals as *International Journal of Qualitative Methods* (Rostvall & West, 2005) and *Philosophy of the Social Sciences* (Matta, 2019) as well as a chapter in *The Routledge Handbook of Multimodal Analysis* (West, 2014). Recently, Kempe and West have collaborated with Gunther Kress's research group on *multimodality* in London, which led to a book publication after Kress's passing (Kress et al., 2021). Kempe and West were interviewed in 2022 for the present publication to develop a better understanding of their corpus of video-based music research across the past twenty years, with particular attention to its inspiration, innovative features, and applications (Kempe & West, 2022).

West noted in the interview that their initial motivation for using video to analyze music teaching was because "[w]e were interested in seeing what was actually going on. We were also interested in what [music teachers and students] were saying, but actually they couldn't say very much" (Kempe & West, 2022). In this context, embodied interactions were more important than verbalizations. Kempe adds that a common attitude among the music teachers they studied was that "[i]t's obvious that this is the way music teaching is done. Why is this interesting?" and that "[t]hey had been teaching for decades without anyone in the room except for themselves and the pupil, so they were not used to talking about their work or traditions . . . people acting within a frozen tradition cannot really talk about it." Kempe credits the work of Ludwik Fleck (1981), who "writes about how one assumes people have a rational explanation for what they are doing, but actually, thinking is *social*. He inspired Kuhn concerning paradigms, and we find he has even more to offer."

Initially, Kempe and West were interested in examining the roles of music teacher and student, but through video they increasingly found that, as Kempe put it, "[t]here was not specific role taking. They constructed each other's roles through their interactions" (Kempe & West, 2022). Several examples illustrate how their methods enabled unique insights that would not otherwise be possible through more traditional approaches to music research. Kempe explained as follows: "Something we noticed very early when we watched videos was that teachers often made sounds and gestures and used their bodies to show they were not content with student actions, so we needed different units to show how the communication occurred." (Kempe & West, 2022)

West also noted that

> when we added the gestures and sounds we could understand it [...] [t]eachers often gave inconsistent or contradictory messages such as looking the other way, or lifting an eyebrow, while commenting on the student's performance. The multimodal transcription revealed such patterns and made it possible to see how the educational interaction was conditioned by subtle communicative cues. Peoples' actions are often guided by institutional practices rather than deliberate assessments. (Kempe & West, 2022)

Indeed, a transcription of only the verbalizations might have been misleading, but through their method Kempe and West were also able to consider how verbalizations compare with observable behavior (including gestures), musical sound (and other sounds produced), and the notated music scores used in the lessons, to produce a more accurate and complete account. In some cases, teacher utterances may be merely out of habit rather than a careful expression of evaluation, which would not be revealed if a researcher relied exclusively on a transcript of verbalizations.

West also mentioned how in one guitar lesson the teacher criticized the student's posture as the reason for poor performance but only later (through stimulated recall) noticed this was exactly the same posture he had been modeling to the student in his own playing (Kempe & West, 2022). These studies also showed that conservatory music teachers sometimes make gestures "toward heaven" when making reference to talent, with the assumption that musical ability is connected to divine will, even traceable to the biblical Parable of the Talents (Matt. 25:14-30).

Ultimately, Kempe and West developed what may be understood as an approach to multiple-reflexive interpretation at different levels of scale: *interpersonal*, *institutional*, and *societal*. As West explains, "[t]his method helps to move responsibility from only individual to also institutional and societal level." This approach would later be enhanced by the notion of *reflexive methodology* advocated by Swedish colleagues (Alvesson & Sköldberg, 2017). Kempe notes how Fleck's theory (1981) aided them in understanding the role of tradition in defining acceptable behaviors and that "[i]n the tradition, inherent talent is an often mentioned explanation for whether a student develops or not" (Kempe & West, 2022).

We will return to Kempe and West's ideas later in this publication, but since the time they began their work, notable music studies to use video and stimulated recall strategies have included doctoral dissertations in Europe on such topics as intensity of interaction in music lessons (Heikinheimo, 2009) and meaning-making processes among young music students (Falthin, 2015) and in North America (Bell, 2013) on interaction with technologies in the music recording process. There have thus far been fewer stimulated recall studies of advanced musicians and situations in which musicians are negotiating between different musical traditions across a cultural divide. Yet stimulated recall methods promise insights in these areas as well, which is where our Element makes its unique contribution. A recent systematic review of the corpus of video-stimulated recall research in education determined it is "a useful method for collecting formal and informal pedagogical experiences to question or even completely transform one's professional thinking and pedagogical actions" (Gazdag, Nagy, & Szivak, 2019, p. 69). We argue the same is true of artistry in music, particularly in intercultural settings. As we will demonstrate in later sections, such techniques engender systematic reflection on contrasting aesthetic systems at a depth of detail that would not otherwise be possible. The research team that developed this publication also participated in studies that made use of video and stimulated recall strategies prior to their intercultural music projects, so by way of conclusion it is useful to consider some of them here.

Initial Stimulated Recall Studies by the Authors

In 2002, Stefan Östersjö made a video-stimulated recall study in collaboration with music education researcher Cecilia Hultberg (2005). The data collection was carried out by making high-quality audio recording and a video recording of each practicing session. The scenario entailed both Hultberg, as an observer, and Östersjö, as a performer, following the score, and Hultberg also taking notes of observations during the session. Videos of the practice sessions would then be viewed in their entirety by Östersjö and Hultberg. Östersjö would comment on the video, and Hultberg would ask additional questions, guided by the notes from her observations. With the aim of taking that approach to a deeper level of analysis, Östersjö turned to the computer-assisted qualitative data analysis software (CAQDAS), HyperRESEARCH, and also adopted an approach to the qualitative analysis building on procedures from grounded theory. This entailed a focus on the use of open coding (Neuman, 2000; Benaquisto, 2008), and, as will be discussed further in Section 3, the possibilities for linking coding with more detailed annotations in the HyperRESEARCH software. Importantly, these procedures sought to acknowledge the parallel processes of musical interpretation through listening and the verbalized analysis, and in which ways these may interact in research on musical creativity (Östersjö, 2008).

Later, Östersjö tested multimodal formats for transcription, using stills from the video and verbal descriptions of action, as a complementary means in the analysis (see Östersjö, 2008, pp. 13–17). In 2006, these experiments with multimodal interpretation and transcription of the content in the video were taken further in additional stimulated recall studies (see Frisk & Östersjö, 2006; Östersjö, 2008). Here, the data consisted of video recordings of Östersjö's collaboration with the Swedish composer Love Mangs in the creation of a new work for plucked string instruments and live electronics. Frisk's role in the study was that of an observer, participating after the data collection. Of importance for the present publication is how this study explored the potential of *multimodal transcription* as a tool for what Liora Bresler (2009) would describe as "making the familiar strange" through its use of theory to engender detachment of the researcher from the data.

While a single artist, researching his or her own practice, must indeed shift between first- and third-person perspectives, the possibilities for enhancing that dynamic between detachment and empathic engagement as a component in the research design was again further explored in a study by Östersjö and colleagues starting in 2014. The aim of the multimodal method in the study was to address pre-reflective and reflective knowledge forms, such as articulated through musical performance, seeking to further enhance the dynamic between observation and empathic engagement. First together and then separately, Gorton, Östersjö, Moelants, and Coorevits identified visual cues from Östersjö's body movements, which they perceived as significant or "expressive" in some way but which were usually not classified as "sound-producing" gestures. These visual cues were named with a code and annotated with reference to the time code, resulting in a rich list of codes from the different perspectives of the performer, composer, and two observers. In conclusion, Gorton and Östersjö (2019) suggest that such study of musical gestures "can thus contribute to an understanding of the tacit domains of performative knowledge in musical practice" (p. 79).

Conclusions

One of the characteristic strengths of video-based stimulated recall research in a field such as music is that it enables performing artists and scholars to find a valuable meeting point between objective and subjective forms of analysis. Indeed, as Frederick Erickson observed, "[i]n looking toward the future, there is no reason to suppose that either the behaviorist or the hermeneutical approaches will achieve total dominance in video research" (Erickson, 2011, p. 186). Rather, we envision a *synergy* between approaches, so research in this field is able to capture not only *observable behaviors*, or only individual *perceptions and experiences*, but rather exactly how these spheres correlate in specific moments in time. As Erickson argued, "there will continue to be a need for hermeneutically oriented video-based research" and for "further development toward maturity in audiovisual imagination," which will lead to "fresh visions of research topics and purposes, as well as of new research techniques" (Erickson, 2011, p. 186). It is particularly in the field of intercultural music collaboration that we seek to offer some "fresh visions" based on this method.

3 Stimulated Recall in the Ensemble Practice of The Six Tones

Stockholm, March 24, 2009

Today we start the second day of rehearsals at EMS. As always, it is such hard work rehearsing the composed pieces. At the end of the day, Trà My and I are mentally exhausted. The notation is so conceptually different in each piece, and nothing is familiar in this music. But also, when we play Tứ Đại Oán, and seek to improvise within and outside its structure, the music, to me, sounds very strange. It feels like I need to distance myself from what I hear in order to find something to play, to contribute. I feel it in my body, every time the piece does not sound like I expected. Already when the ornamentation in the guitar doesn't follow the rules of the mode, my listening is disturbed, but most often, my reactions are to do with the electronics.

– Nguyễn Thanh Thủy

In March 2009, The Six Tones were rehearsing at Electronic Music Studios (EMS) in Stockholm, preparing for a tour in Sweden and Denmark, organized by Concerts Sweden, a national organization for touring productions. On the program were several traditional Vietnamese pieces, played in the hybrid setting of *đàn tranh*, *đàn bầu*, and ten-string guitar, along with several premieres of new compositions by Swedish composers Kent Olofsson, Malin Bång, Henrik Denerin, and Love Mangs. The program also included Henrik Frisk's composition "The Six Tones." Many of these pieces served as a framework for experimentation with different types of group improvisation, an approach that had become a central method in the intercultural collaborations developed by the ensemble. But in an intercultural music group like The Six Tones, improvisation can refer to multiple kinds of practices. In traditional Vietnamese music a piece is best understood as a structure for improvisation, within a given framework. Particularly in *Đờn Ca Tài Tử*,[8] a form of chamber music from the south of Vietnam, each piece is preceded by a *Rao*, an improvised part that both introduces the key of the song and sets its mood. These forms of idiomatic improvisation, particular to Vietnamese tradition, were contrasted by approaches to "free" or "non-idiomatic" (Bailey, 1992) improvisation.

In the rehearsals at EMS, the friction between these many different practices and individual musical *voices* (see Section 1) surfaced in different ways. Time was limited, since the rehearsals took place only a few days before the beginning of the tour. As is often the case, many of the scores to be premiered were delivered immediately before the rehearsals. For the two Vietnamese members of the group, already the nature of the contemporary Western notation, sometimes with extended techniques and other recent innovations, was as unfamiliar as the musical idioms they represented. But, artistically, one of the greatest challenges was to develop ways of improvising, which would allow transitions between traditional Vietnamese music and "free" improvisation. As early as 2007, The Six Tones set out to do this in a performance of *Tứ Đại Oán*, a piece central in *Đờn Ca Tài Tử*, performed with *đàn tranh*, ten-string guitar and live electronics. In the EMS rehearsals, the same three players, Henrik, Stefan and Thủy, sought ways of stylistically integrating unusually diverse materials for performance as a coherent whole.

In intercultural music-making, the development of a shared voice is a central challenge (see also Nguyễn & Östersjö, 2019; Östersjö, 2020). This section seeks to trace the artistic processes of negotiating voice in the rehearsals and the concert performances that followed, with particular interest in how this work eventually led to the making of *Signal in Noise* (The Six Tones, 2013), an album recorded in Hà Nội in April 2010, in which idiomatic Vietnamese and "self-idiomatic"

---

[8] At the end of the nineteenth century, a new form of chamber music emerged in the south of Vietnam, most often referred to as *Đờn Ca Tài Tử*. An important factor was that musicians of *Ca Nhạc Huế*, a form of traditional music centered around the royal court in Huế, migrated south at the end of the nineteenth century. Performers of *Ca Nhạc Huế* were rarely professional musicians but rather higher officials or members of the royal family (Lê, 2003). A possible motivation for migrating to the south may have been the political aim of the Nguyễn dynasty to reunite the country, but it is also possible that some of these musicians were migrating as a response to the gradual decline of the royal court in Huế. Either way, and more importantly for the purposes of this chapter, these musicians brought a tradition of skilled and highly informed "amateur" performance, and also a history of internal migration, through their journey south. Further, they were part of an anti-French movement across the country, wherein Confucianism became a symbol of the fight against colonialism. This led many intellectuals to leave the cities, seeking to lead a life according to traditional values in the countryside (Lê, 2003).

improvisational practices came together. An important feature of the album was also that it was built on many guest appearances from the music scene in Hà Nội, and various leading artists from the experimental and traditional music scene also contributed, always with very little, or no, opportunity for rehearsal. When recording the album, it became apparent that The Six Tones had established a shared voice, which seemed to enable the group to function as a platform for intercultural collaboration. Here we will offer an analysis of this artistic develop-ment and the role that the listening practice of stimulated recall may have had in this process.

Coding and Re-coding the Recordings

In 2009, The Six Tones became part of an international artistic research project called (re)thinking Improvisation, its role being to complete a subproject on the use of improvisation in intercultural collaboration and also in the context of traditional Vietnamese music. Hence, when gathering after the tour to review the documentation from rehearsals and concert performances, collected in March and April of 2009, the ensemble's focus was on improvised sections of the music. This entailed compositions that rested substantially on improvisation or the study of improvised introductions, the *Rao*, in traditional Vietnamese pieces. It also included some examples of performances that would seek to weave free improvisation together with performance of traditional Vietnamese music, as in performances of *Tứ Đại Oán* (introduced earlier). All sequences from recordings of both rehearsals and performances that featured improvisa-tion in pieces like these were identified and parsed into separate clips for careful analysis. Stimulated recall sessions were set up, often organized in pairs, but sometimes in groups of three, depending for instance on the need for translation in the verbal interactions between performers, using these clips as sources. Indeed, a fundamental challenge for the team in making this analysis was that of working in a second or third language for the coding of qualitative data. Translation between Vietnamese and English was frequently necessary, and fluency varied between the participants – Ngô Trà My being the least fluent in English and Thủy sometimes playing the role of interpreter from Vietnamese – as well as responding to the stimuli. Linguistic differences also made the analysis into a constant reconsider-ation of nuance in the various languages: Vietnamese, Swedish, and English.

On a suggestion from Stefan, who introduced methods for analysis that he had used in previous studies, The Six Tones decided to formalize their analysis by making open coding of the video documentation. For the group, a central motivation was to avoid preconceived understandings and thereby aim to counteract what has come to be known as "colonizing" perspectives. This, however, was not a given, but rather a possibility afforded by the use of stimulated recall through open-coding procedures, while this research design in turn demanded a constant awareness of the challenges and pitfalls in the analytical process. The coding was made directly from the video, and the use of verbatim transcription was limited to situations identified as potentially significant. Tracing the interactions and analyzing them further through the use of stimulated recall methods allowed the group to go beyond the immediate observations represented earlier to a deeper level of collective reflection.

The basic procedure was to review the clip from the beginning and stop the playback at any moment in which anyone in the group found that something attracted their attention. A sequence would be identified, marked in the software, and given a code. The negotiation of codes normally continued throughout the sessions and across different clips, but an essential aim was to seek consensus in the group and thereby create an intersubjective understanding of each set of observations. A selected sequence would be given several codes and then further described and defined by free-text annotations to document additional reflections.

As schematically described in Figure 2, stimulated recall using a video recording with musical content entails the activation of several simultaneous processes of listening, verbalized intersubjective reflection, and analysis. The arrow on the right side refers to processes of musical interpretation, described by Östersjö (2008, 2017) as *thinking-through-listening*. In the present scenario, these are processes that rest on the embodied knowledge of a performer, drawing on countless hours of rehearsal and performance and largely operating in a nonverbal domain. We draw attention to the fact that each individual tends to shift between first- and third-person perspectives. Moreover, a large proportion of the sessions tend to be dominated by a second-person, intersubjective dialogue, typically when negotiating the formulation of codes and annotations. Such verbal interactions also serve to connect each musician's thinking-through-listening with a conceptual understanding of the phenomena, thereby directly grounding the analysis in shared listenings.

We will in the following section provide a detailed description of how the method for jointly coding and annotating the videos developed throughout the work of the ensemble in 2009–10. For this purpose, we will consider coding and annotations during two separate sessions, carried out by Henrik, Stefan, and Thùy in the spring of 2009 and 2010, respectively. The analysis was applied to the same clip, drawn from a recording made during the rehearsals at EMS on March 24, 2009.[9] Here,

---

[9] All video examples are found in the following link: www.researchcatalogue.net/view/1301475/1302132.

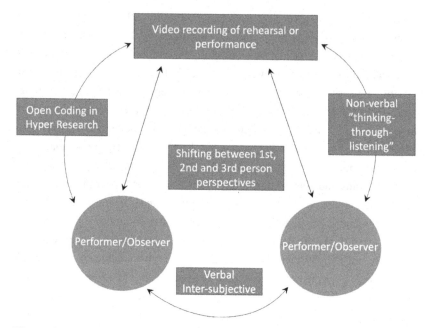

Figure 2 A representation of a typical stimulated recall scenario in the sessions with The Six Tones

Henrik, Stefan, and Thủy were rehearsing *Tứ Đại Oán*, using the agreed structure, which divided the piece into three parts, with different forms of improvisation in the opening (Improv. 1), a middle section (Improv. 2), and the final section of the piece (Improv. 3). For the purposes of the stimulated recall analysis, all instances of these three parts were edited into separate video clips, which were played back using HyperRESEARCH software and viewed together by the team. A basic prerequisite for understanding computer-aided qualitative analysis is that the architecture of the software has a particular impact on the structuring and analysis of the material. As mentioned in Section 2, in HyperRESEARCH, codes and annotations are clearly linked, and these two levels of analysis can in turn be structured in individual cases. These structural features support a qualitative analysis in which annotations are written in an analytical and reflective manner, affording the possibility of including such jointly negotiated text in the final writing of a paper or book chapter. In order to establish stimulated recall methods that contribute to decolonization of music research, it is important for interpretations and coding to be developed collabora-tively within the intercultural research team. It can be a challenge to establish procedures for how best to maintain the content of the collaborative analysis, but we find the joint formulation of annotations, which can be immediately brought into the writing, to be a great advantage.

Through the team's repeated stimulated recall sessions following this procedure, a shared understanding of different attitudes of performing began to emerge, observable through the codes and annotations. Two overarching themes were *interaction* and *initiative*, which became the headings of one of the first cases. Within this heading, the group mapped individual initiatives (with codes referencing an individual's "playing"), while also making observations of how the interaction was driven by attitudes to performing, characterized as different modes of *listening*.

In Figure 3, we have plotted all codes and annotations in a timeline, which represents the first 45 seconds of a selected clip analyzed in the two different coding sessions (2009 and 2010). As can be seen, in the 2009 session, only one code was selected (searching listening), and the annotation is rather brief and generic at the same time, considering the whole 45 seconds as one event. The 2010 session, however, is far more detailed, segmenting the clip into multiple layers. Two codes address initiatives, with reference to Henrik's first entry using high-pitched electronics (commented also in the annotation from 2009), as well as Stefan's attempt to continue the percussive materials from the transition "as a response to Thủy's melodic motif." This was given the code "failed expectation" since "it was not picked up by anyone." All the other codes refer to interaction through different modes of listening. While in the 2009 session code list, only three modes were established as codes (attentive, failed, and searching listening, out of which only two are present in these examples), in 2010, we also find the modalities of structural and integrated listening. It may be important to note how all codes signify directedness in various configurations and that the annotations seek to further clarify in which way one or more performers engage in a certain mode of listening. Hence, the stimulated recall analysis concerns a relational perspective on musical listening, as well as agencies at play.

What appears to be the burning question, then, is when looking at the coding from a year later, how would it be possible for a musician to listen in several different ways simultaneously as the graphical representation of the coding suggests? In order to address this question, we will consider each modality separately and how their interaction is described in the annotations. Starting with *integrated listening*, it is described as "taking the material further in a similar manner" in two instruments or interacting "in the same sonic sphere." Such attitudes of performing could also be described as "blending" and are typical of some forms of interaction in improvisation. *Attentive listening* is described as an immediate response to initiative and as smooth interaction within the group. *Structural* is described in a more conceptual manner, seemingly with the aim of capturing the multifaceted nature of perception in musical performance and how listening contributes to the continuous shaping of musical

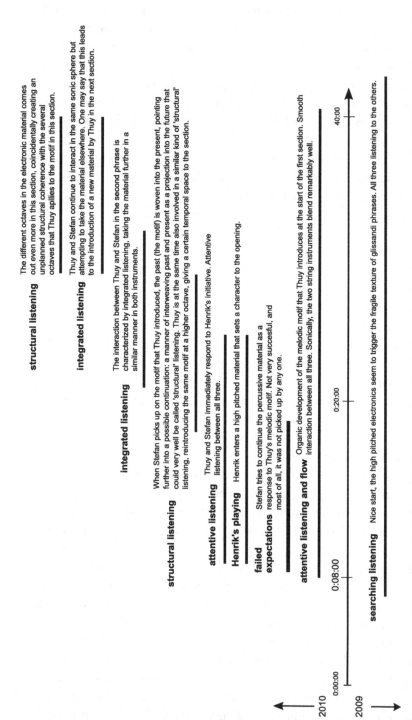

structural listening — The different octaves in the electronic material comes out even more in this section, coincidentally creating an unplanned structural coherence with the several octaves that Thuy apllies to the motif in this section.

integrated listening — Thuy and Stefan continue to interact in the same sonic sphere but attempting to take the material elsewhere. One may say that this leads to the introduction of a new material by Thuy in the next section.

integrated listening — The interaction between Thuy and Stefan in the second phrase is characterized by integrated listening, taking the material further in a similar manner in both instruments.

structural listening — When Stefan picks up on the motif that Thuy introduced, the past (the motif) is woven into the present, pointing further into a possible continuation: a manner of interweaving past and present as a projection into the future that could very well be called 'structural' listening. Thuy is at the same time also involved in a similar kind of 'structural' listening, reintroducing the same motif at a higher octave, giving a certain temporal space to the section.

attentive listening — Thuy and Stefan immediately respond to Henrik's initiative. Attentive listening between all three.

Henrik's playing — Henrik enters a high pitched material that sets a character to the opening.

failed expectations — Stefan tries to continue the percussive material as a response to Thuy's melodic motif. Not very successful, and most of all, it was not picked up by any one.

attentive listening and flow — Organic development of the melodic motif that Thuy introduces at the start of the first section. Smooth interaction between all three. Sonically, the two string instruments blend remarkably well.

searching listening — Nice start, the high pitched electronics seem to trigger the fragile texture of glissandi phrases. All three listening to the others.

0:00:00   0:08:00   0:20:00   0:40:00

2010

2009

Figure 3 A display of the sections that were coded and annotated in the two stimulated recall sessions in spring 2009 and spring 2010 respectively. The video under analysis was recorded on March 24 (see video example 1 in research catalogue [RC]). The line under each set of code and annotation indicates the duration of the selected segment. This figure displays the analysis in the first 45 seconds

form. But how then do these different forms of listening align in the flow of the performance? Looking at the temporal organization of these codes, it can be observed that a first instance of two codes of attentive listening leads to the development of material. The first code refers to the organic growth of melodic material, which continues through the end of the clip. The second, shorter coded section refers specifically to how Stefan and Thùy respond to Henrik's first initiative. These two processes are further developed through the subsequent *structural listening*, expressed in Stefan's playing, through which the melodic material is taken further. These two approaches (the *attentive* and *structural listening*) lead to the following coded section of *integrated listening* in the interplay between Thùy and Stefan. This interaction is taken in a new direction, described by the dual codes of a different form of *integrated listening*, aligning with a new expression of *structural listening*. From this synthesis emerges a rather logical musical structure starting out with an early development of material that is structured, further developed, and integrated.

As pointed out by Nguyễn and Östersjö (2013) it is important to underline how the aim of this analytical approach was neither to identify absolute characteristics of musical listening – like Adorno's (1989) prescriptive typology of listeners[10] – nor to offer a music-theoretical analysis of what was played. The intention "when defining these codes was to map our embodied knowing as performers and listeners" (p. 198) and hence, "the series of modalities of listening that form the basis for the analysis refer to our own subjective understandings and do not have an aim beyond constituting a description of the musical interaction" (Adorno, 1989, p. 198).

It is of methodological importance to note how, when the group continued their analysis by re-coding the same materials, the nature of these annotations changed. Structural listening became an important category in the further development of the analysis. When used in 2009, there was no detailed discussion of the concept, and its meaning seems to be taken for granted in the annotations (see the annotation to attentive listening in the 2009 coding in Figure 4). But in spring 2010 the structural listening code received a more considered set of commentary. Here, phenomenologically speaking, one can observe how, in the flow of the improvisation, a performer may "weave past and present as a projection into the future" as phrased in the following annotation:

> When Stefan picks up on the motif that Thùy introduced, the past (the motif) is woven into the present, pointing further into a possible continuation: a manner of interweaving past and present as a projection into the future

---

[10] For an extension of Adorno's typology to world music listeners, see the section "The Taste for the Other" in Laurent Aubert's *The Music of the Other* (2007, pp. 43–46).

that could very well be called "structural" listening. Thủy is at the same time involved in a similar kind of "structural" listening, reintroducing the same motif at a higher octave, giving a certain temporal space to the section. (Stimulated Recall Annotation, 2010)

In the stimulated recall analysis, the group not only analyzed the artistically successful interactions but also sought to understand shortcomings, mistakes, and misunderstandings. In Figure 3 we find the code *failed expectations*, in which the annotation identifies a moment in which an unsuccessful initiative from Stefan is not picked up by anyone and therefore results in failed expectations. A recurring code was *failed listening*, which is found in Figure 4. The annotation describes how "Thủy and Stefan try in different ways to create a crescendo with the current material but this fails, several times. Neither initiative is picked up in the right moment." These analyses of relative failure, thereby supporting the identification of successful interactions through the codes of attentive, searching, integrated, and structural listening, appears to us to have been useful, forming part of the artistic development within the group.

But what is the nature of these more conceptually driven analytical observations? We would argue that in these instances, rather than enabling the participating performers to merely relive the original situation (as was initially thought to be the aim of stimulated recall), a more convincing understanding of the listening situation is that of a form of phenomenological variation, as we propose in Section 1. Such an analytical process should consider the temporal nature of lived experience. As observed by Vermersch (1999, p. 32) this may be understood as a series of phenomenological reductions through which the subject, first "alone or with a mediator, tries to describe his lived experience," an undertaking that takes shape as *living through another lived experience* (see Figure 1,). Through this second lived experience, access to a reflexive understanding may be gained, enabling the subject to "describe what he thereby becomes conscious of" (p. 33). Vermersch (1999) concludes that "in other words, one must first have practised introspection ... in order to make of it an object of study and so to practise an introspection of an introspection" (pp. 32–33).

Vermersch (1999) describes the thought sequence from introspection to meta-reflection in a linear manner, developed through consecutive lived experiences. While Vermersch's conceptualization is generally useful, we find that the listening processes of stimulated recall do not necessarily unfold as a linear progression toward greater abstraction. Looking at the documentation of stimulated recall sessions with The Six Tones, it is rather a matter of exploring different phenomenological variations on the same material, wherein the listener may adopt varying positions in relation to the stimulus. Furthermore, and

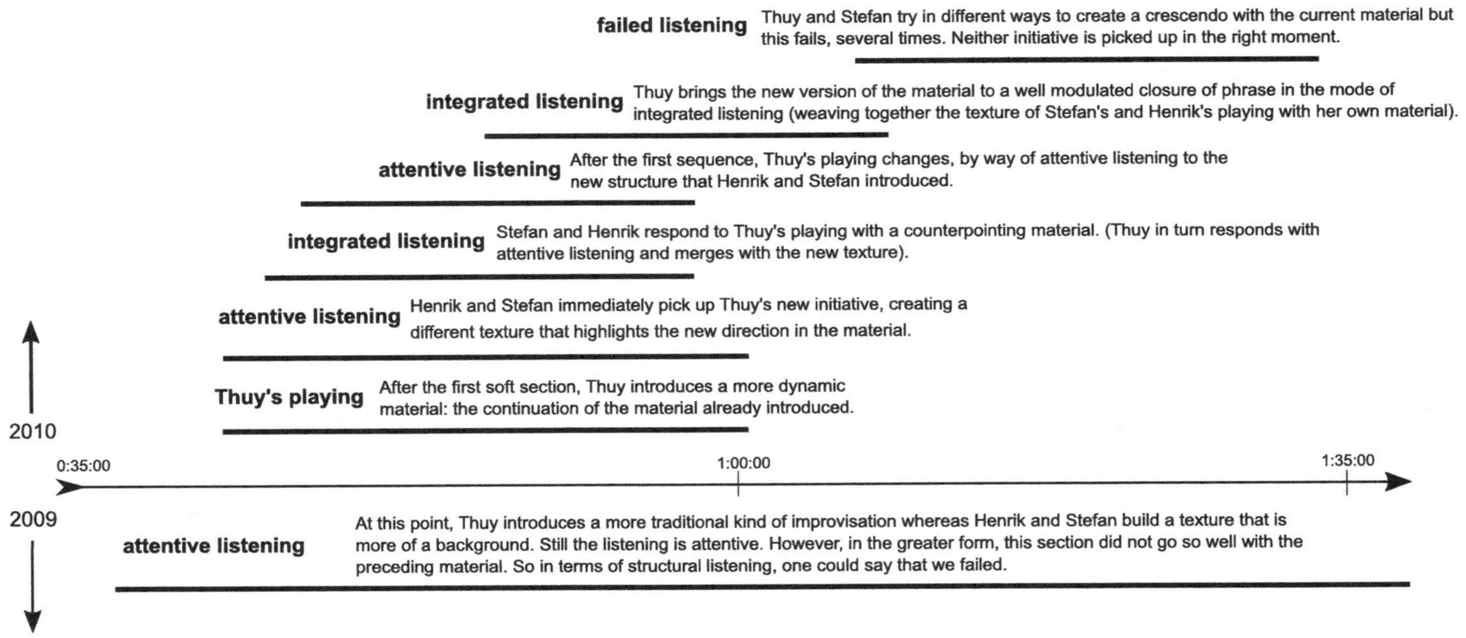

failed listening — Thuy and Stefan try in different ways to create a crescendo with the current material but this fails, several times. Neither initiative is picked up in the right moment.

integrated listening — Thuy brings the new version of the material to a well modulated closure of phrase in the mode of integrated listening (weaving together the texture of Stefan's and Henrik's playing with her own material).

attentive listening — After the first sequence, Thuy's playing changes, by way of attentive listening to the new structure that Henrik and Stefan introduced.

integrated listening — Stefan and Henrik respond to Thuy's playing with a counterpointing material. (Thuy in turn responds with attentive listening and merges with the new texture).

attentive listening — Henrik and Stefan immediately pick up Thuy's new initiative, creating a different texture that highlights the new direction in the material.

Thuy's playing — After the first soft section, Thuy introduces a more dynamic material: the continuation of the material already introduced.

attentive listening — At this point, Thuy introduces a more traditional kind of improvisation whereas Henrik and Stefan build a texture that is more of a background. Still the listening is attentive. However, in the greater form, this section did not go so well with the preceding material. So in terms of structural listening, one could say that we failed.

1:35:00

1:00:00

0:35:00

2010

2009

Figure 4 A display of the sections that were coded and annotated in the two stimulated recall sessions in spring 2009 and spring 2010, respectively. The video under analysis was recorded on March 24. The line under each set of code and annotation indicates the duration of the selected segment

as discussed in Section 1, in the making of stimulated recall analysis, the intentionality of the technology itself must also be taken into account (Krueger, 2014).

In 2012, while preparing material for a book chapter based on the aforementioned (re)thinking Improvisation study, we revisited the material that had been coded in 2009 and 2010. A new stimulated recall analysis of the same video material was then enhanced by a longitudinal study of recordings of the same piece, *Tứ Đại Oán*, drawn from concert performances in 2007, 2009, and 2011. Our objective in expanding the range of materials was to capture the artistic development of the group across time. As part of this analysis, we further elaborated on the codes used, specifically those concerned with modes of listening. The definitions drawn from the analysis made in the 2010 round of coding (see Figures 3 and 4 for a sample) were further detailed and refined through both the third round of coding and the longitudinal study carried out in 2012.[11] This set of definitions served to clarify the different modalities at play in the interaction. They lay the ground for the first comprehensive analysis of the impact, which the intercultural collaboration had had on the individual performers, as well as on the group, as a collaborative entity. Judging from the development of these definitions, the process of re-coding the videos appears to have afforded a deepened level of reflection and analysis.

If, during the first three years, The Six Tones regarded their collaboration as an exchange between performers of traditional Vietnamese music on the one hand and Western experimental music on the other, by 2010 a different understanding had emerged, in which the group was first and foremost thought of as a player on the experimental music scene in Vietnam. It was a formative experience for the group to take part in (and co-organize) the Hanoi New Music Meeting in 2009, curated by Vietnamese composer Trần Thị Kim Ngọc. This was the first time that the group performed together with other improvisers and composers on the Vietnamese scene, and the kinship was very striking and immediate. Similar experiences followed when the group played for the first time at the Hanoi Sound Stuff Festival in 2010, curated by DJ and improviser Trí Minh.[12] These artistic projects, together with the established routine of rehearsal and stimulated recall analysis, formed part of an artistic development, which culminated in the making of a double album eventually titled *Signal in Noise*. This CD was recorded in Hà Nội in April 2010. The concept of the album was to invite leading artists from the traditional and experimental music scenes in Hà Nội for an exploration of the different forms

---

[11] For a detailed account of these definitions, see Östersjö and Nguyễn (2013, p. 195).

[12] For an account of the history of experimental music and sound art in Vietnam see Nguyễn and Östersjö (2021).

of improvisation that these different musical cultures embrace. It was part of the album's concept that the recordings were to be made with little or no rehearsal time. Hence, compared to the laborious work of The Six Tones, when developing forms for improvising in *Tứ Đại Oán*, the entire CD would be recorded in less time than that used for rehearsals in preparation for the tour in spring 2009.

One point of comparison could be two tracks on the CD that were recorded with the traditional Vietnamese flutist Lê Phổ, in interaction with Stefan playing ten-string guitar and Henrik playing live electronics.[13] Hence, this entailed the same setup as performances of *Tứ Đại Oán*, only replacing one traditional musician with another. What is perhaps most striking here is that the CD recordings were preceded by only one rehearsal of about 20 minutes. The recording session comprised three takes, also made in 20 minutes each. These recordings became a defining component of the CD and have returned in later productions, as when the recordings for *Signal in Noise* became material in making the music for *Forgetting Vietnam* together with the filmmaker Trịnh Minh-ha.[14] Similarly, other sessions brought the group together with Trí Minh and Vũ Nhật Tân, in recordings that began to establish a new sound in the group featuring more electric guitar and saxophone, along with layers of noise and field recordings, thereby incorporating elements that were typical of the experimental music scene in Vietnam at the time. A general feature of all these recording sessions is the ease with which artistic collaboration developed, and we believe that most of all, this was the result of The Six Tones having developed into a platform for intercultural dialogue, a context within which new voices could easily be integrated. We believe that the detailed analysis of improvised interactions enabled through stimulated recall created an awareness of each performer's agency and also of various artistic methods that can contribute to the weaving together of heterogeneous voices (see also Nguyễn & Östersjö, 2019). However, in 2019, we still felt that the longitudinal analysis, initiated in 2012, had not yet produced a conclusive understanding of the processes.

Analytical Approaches toward a Deepened Understanding

The data collected from the work of the group was extremely rich, and although repeated analysis of the video recordings had provided increasing insight, in 2019, The Six Tones set out to develop a meta-perspective using different analytical techniques. Here, Östersjö and Nguyễn coded all the annotations

---

[13] See also the discussion in Nguyễn and Östersjö (2012) concerning the interactions with Lê Phổ.
[14] The latest release including parts of the recording with Lê Phổ was a remix of a track by the Ethernet Orchestra, released on Pablo Nuevo in January 2022.

from previous studies in 2009, 2010, and 2012, now working mainly with text documents exported from HyperRESEARCH. The entire text material (all annotations from all previous stimulated recall sessions) was coded using two different analytical grids. Thereafter, selected clips, which had attracted attention in the new coding, served as the basis for renewed stimulated recall analysis. The coding of all of the annotations used two analytical grids. In the first clip, The Six Tones identified generative and selective processes in the interaction, following a model proposed by Johnson-Laird (2002). In the second analysis, the same text was re-coded, now with the aim of understanding the development of voice. To demonstrate the outcome of the second round of coding we can revisit Figure 4, and the code *integrated listening* at 45 seconds into the clip. In the original annotation from 2010, the first observation was that "Stefan and Henrik respond to Thùy's playing with a counterpointing material." This sentence was now coded as an example of "heterogeneous voice." The next annotation from 2010 was *attentive listening*, starting 2 seconds later, in which it was noted how "after the first sequence, Thùy's playing changes, by way of attentive listening to the new structure that Henrik and Stefan introduced," an approach that was now coded as *blending*. In an annotation in the 2019 coding, which reexamined a recording of *Tứ Đại Oán* from 2007, Thùy agreed with the previous annotation, observing how she was continually in a mode of "searching listening," but now noted that "what we failed to see in the previous analysis is how this is also due to a search for a new voice" (Östersjö, 2020, p. 99). Thùy then concluded that "at this point in 2007, I had not developed means to interact with the music that Henrik and Stefan created through this encounter with *Tứ Đại Oán*" (Östersjö, 2020, p. 99). For the purposes of the current section, it may suffice to say that this analysis has further clarified the processes of negotiating voice in intercultural collaboration.[15]

However, conceived specifically for *artistic research* purposes by the group, it would be a mistake to see the method of stimulated recall as primarily aiming for the production of discursive analysis, that is, the coding and annotations. The repeated cycles of playing-reflecting-analyzing that have been part of the practice of The Six Tones have allowed the group to develop a decolonized aesthetic framework that depends more on the intercultural practice of the group and its musical preconditions than it does on existing stylistic measures. This has further made possible an inclusive relation to the projects the group has engaged with and, although it is not possible to exclusively relate this to the conscious development of stimulated recall practices, it has certainly improved

---

[15] The study provided material for *Listening to the Other* (Östersjö, 2008), where a further discussion of the method's impact on the artistic development of the group can be found.

our artistic development in this direction. In the artistic research of the Six Tones, the focus is instead on how stimulated recall creates a new practice within the group that is enhanced through the method: A transformed listening. Verbalizing and signifying the experience of repeated listening and reflection is an important part of the process but not the only final goal. Rather, it is also this transformed listening, which among other things has enabled modes of inter-action beyond cultural prejudice with musical Others, which in itself was the deepest aim.

Summary

We found evidence that the use of stimulated recall contributed to the ensemble's artistic development by increasing awareness of artistic challenges and creating situations for shared listenings. The analytical approach was based on intersubjective negotiation of meaning, articulated through qualitative research procedures of coding and annotating recordings of rehearsals and concert performances. By repeatedly re-coding the same material and also adding a text-based analysis of all annotations, further analytical observations were enabled. The analysis of the repeated coding, presented in this section, shows how shared listenings provided different forms of understanding at different levels of resolution in the observations.

4 Musical Transformations: Sharing the Method with Others

Nha Trang, June 2, 2012

This evening Thủy and I walked across the Trần Phú bridge and continued along Cù Huân street. We entered a small, local restaurant along the waterfront with very few customers. In a corner of the restaurant, a group of musicians were seated around a table, engaged in a performance that appeared not to be intended for an audience, and went on for hours. One of them played electric Vietnamese guitar, through a tiny amp, and the others took turns singing. A traditional piece called Vọng Cổ was played, time after time, in different versions, each time with a new singer. Between these versions, they turned to folk songs or Nhạc Vàng (Yellow Music), but Vọng Cổ kept returning. When walking back to the hotel, the idea of a recording project with The Six Tones began to emerge. How could such variations around the same piece be turned into a more experimental form, with Vọng Cổ continuously returning, but each time in a new shape?

– Stefan Östersjö

The year 2012 was a busy time for The Six Tones. The ensemble worked in Vietnam during several periods, particularly with the premiere of the perform-ance art installation Inside/Outside in the Chèo theatre in Hà Nội in November. In this work, two traditional Vietnamese pieces, *Dạ Cổ Hoài Lang* and *Vọng Cổ*, were performed and also transformed, serving as material for experimental improvisations. A central method for these transformations was to allow choreographic movements to inspire new developments in the music.[16] Later, after premiering a choreographed version of *Chuyển Dịch* by Trần Thị Kim Ngọc in a temple in Hà Nội, Nguyễn and Östersjö traveled south. Upon reaching the city of Nha Trang, they came across a local performance of *Vọng Cổ*, and the initial ideas for a CD project centered around this piece, and its many variants began to emerge. They soon realized that this album would need to be built around encounters with master performers of *Vọng Cổ* from the south. Nguyễn had previously studied with several leading masters of the *đàn tranh* in the south, which was helpful when Nguyễn and Östersjö traveled to the Mekong Delta in 2014 to meet the master of the *đàn kìm* and Vietnamese guitar, Thiện Vũ, with the aim of inviting him to join the project. They started planning for recordings to be made in the following year, but this first attempt at the project was abruptly interrupted by the passing of Thiện Vũ. The final structure of the project did not materialize until 2018, when it was further developed into a research project that would seek to explore the history of this music, as well as its present-day performance practice.

Summary of Project Structure and Aims

Between 2018 and 2022, The Six Tones, together with David Hebert, carried out a research project titled Musical Transformations, funded by the Swedish Marcus and Amalia Wallenberg Foundation (MAW). The aim of the project was to develop new knowledge and deepen understanding of processes for renewal of musical practices in intercultural and transnational contexts, taking an example from traditional music in the south of Vietnam. Musical Transformations sought to bring methods from artistic research and ethnomusicology together with the further aim of addressing the methodological challenge of the emic/etic problem.

The artistic content is built around the traditions associated with a prominent song called *Vọng Cổ*, which had developed from another song, *Dạ Cổ Hoài Lang*, composed by Sáu Lầu in 1920 (Cannon 2012; Trainor, 1975).[17] There were several reasons for dedicating the project to a study of a single notable

---

[16] Conceptually, the piece sought to develop a critique of the gendered gesture, which has become typical of traditional Vietnamese music performance, particularly as developed in TV shows (Nguyễn, 2019), and the choreography in Inside/Outside was created from an analysis of such gestures. For a further discussion of this project, see Nguyễn (2019).

[17] It is challenging to offer a reliable history of *Vọng Cổ* since documentation is scarce, very much due to the fact that Vietnam was in a state of civil war during the major part of its further development. For a more detailed discussion, see Östersjö (2022).

piece. Much like examples that are likely to be familiar to international readers – such as George Gershwin's "I Got Rhythm" modeling the "rhythm changes" chords at the root of most Bebop tunes in jazz or even the form of Pachelbel's Canon as a basis for American pop songs in the 1970s and 1980s – *Vọng Cổ* had become a profoundly influential piece in the contemporary canon of Vietnamese traditional music. Since the 1920s, the song had undergone an intricate development, whereby not only the musical structures were expanded, but it also evolved into the cornerstone of *Cải Lương*, a popular form of music theatre (Trainor, 1975, Nguyễn, 2010). Furthermore, this music emerged through a particular interaction between traditional Vietnamese music traditions and a series of other influences, most importantly, from Western popular music, which was ubiquitous in the urban colonial center of Sài Gòn through the early twentieth century (DeWald, 2012).

The process through which the structure of *Vọng Cổ* was expanded can be traced back to 1925, when the composer Trịnh Thiên Tư created a version of *Dạ Cổ Hoài Lang* where each *Câu* (phrase) was extended to four bars (Huỳnh, 2016). This version remained popular for a long time, but in 1937, a piece actually titled *Vọng Cổ* was recorded for the first time on the Asia label with the singer Năm Nghĩa. In this recording, the melodic framework of *Dạ Cổ Hoài Lang* had been expanded to eight bars per *Câu* (a version henceforth referred to as *Vọng Cổ* 8). This extended structure allowed the performers a greater window for improvisation, with the melody serving as a melodic framework for such improvised performance. In 1938, the first recording of *Vọng Cổ* 16 was released, again on the Asia label (Kiều, 1997). Only in the 1950s, an even more extended version was introduced: *Vọng Cổ* 32. Since this time, the twenty phrases of *Dạ Cổ Hoài Lang* were no longer used in their entirety, and the number of phrases was typically reduced to no more than six.

The Musical Transformations project limited its focus to instrumental performance of *Vọng Cổ*, leaving vocal and staged performance aside. The project aimed both to document the history of sociomusical change, which has transformed the *Vọng Cổ*, and to explore its present-day potential for further renewal. This was achieved by instigating experimentation with its musical materials and performance practices through intercultural collaboration with some of the leading masters of the tradition. Hence, Musical Transformations entailed a radically experimental music project, which actively engaged master performers of traditional Vietnamese music in intercultural collaboration with experimental music, incorporating practices of live electronics and free improvisation, while simultaneously documenting the heritage of their traditional performance practices. The final artistic outcome is a double CD, which combines the legacy of the *Vọng Cổ* tradition with experimental versions of the piece, created through experimental intercultural musicianship. At the same time, the form of the album is also inspired by how *Vọng Cổ* is commonly played in extended cycles wherein a version of the piece is interrupted by a pop song or folk melody, after which the performers return to the main piece.

The study of musical change can be divided into what Nettl terms "historical ethnomusicology" on the one hand and studies of the impact of globalization in traditional and urban cultures on the other (Nettl, 2005). In ethnomusicology "bi-musicality" (Hood, 1960) is an important methodological feature, seeking to include "insider" perspectives, as well as the "music knowledge of music" that Seeger discusses (Hood, 1971, p. vii). Such approaches, although critiqued and developed further in different ways, have remained central to ethnomusicology, emphasizing thereby the musical learning and performing competence of the researcher, as a means to create an understanding, which is based on musical knowing and not merely on observation and analysis (Cottrell, 2007; Solís, 2004). A central dispute has been whether a focus on performative approaches may obscure a rich socioculturally grounded analysis. A challenge has been how to access the situated knowledge of the "insider," while also preserving the "outsider" perspective's possibilities for knowledge construction and how to make these operations transparent in the research design (Nettl, 2005). Throughout the various phases of musical performance, ethnography, and stimulated recall-based coding of video in lab sessions, the aim of Musical Transformations has been to create a practice building on "a double reflexivity, that oscillates between emic and etic roles, between actor-activist and observer-companion perspectives, that continually challenges the conceptualizations and 'implicit theories' of either type of participant" (Dietz, 2011, p. 14). Musical Transformations sought to develop a decolonizing methodology, which involves local cultural bearers in collaborative research projects. This method development builds on the use of stimulated recall analysis, involving *all* participating artists and researchers. It emphasizes shared listenings and intersubjectively negotiated understanding, enabling a double reflexivity that aims for postcolonial awareness (Smith, 2012).

The method of stimulated recall – such as it has been developed as a method for the study of intercultural collaboration in the practice of The Six Tones – was shared with an extended group of performers in a recording project, as we sought to understand their intentions, preferences, and creative choices through intersubjective dialogue. Hence, the aim of this section is to describe and evaluate our use of stimulated recall methods in order to assess their potential for decolonizing music research methods.

Timeline of Project 2018–19

Musical Transformations had a head start in August 2018, a few months before the official launch of the project, when Östersjö and Nguyễn traveled in the Mekong Delta to meet musicians, make recordings of different versions of *Vọng Cổ*, and complete stimulated recall interviews with each performer they encountered. The aim with this field trip was first and foremost to identify a group of musicians with whom the core work of the project – development of a double album documenting traditional *Vọng Cổ* heritage interwoven with recordings of experimental music – could be successfully completed. Although a number of skilled musicians were recorded during this first trip, the performers who eventually became our main collaborators were not brought into the project until October of the same year. A challenge that had to be addressed was finding a guitarist who could replace Thiện Vũ, who had passed away. For the recording project we decided to work with three master musicians, who also were the core members of a traditional Vietnamese music group and often performed as a trio, typically also with one or more singers. There is an interesting dynamic in this ensemble we selected, which may be partly related to its generational spread. Phạm Công Tỵ, who plays two kinds of two-stringed fiddle, the *đàn gáo* and *đàn cò*,[18] is the oldest member of the trio. Phạm Văn Môn is a leading performer of the Vietnamese guitar, and he recorded with Phạm Công Tỵ for the first time on an album released in 1998. The youngest member of their group, Huỳnh Tuấn, plays the *đàn kìm*. Since all three musicians lived in Sài Gòn (Hồ Chí Minh City), southern Vietnam's great metropolis, most working sessions were carried out in studios in this city.

The stimulated recall sessions carried out in August 2018 became important for the design of our subsequent work. Here, Östersjö and Nguyễn piloted the same method as that previously used by The Six Tones: Each performer would record several versions of *Vọng Cổ* and then again meet up with the two researchers to review their recordings, which were discussed and analyzed through a process of open coding (see Section 3). However, already during the first working day, the two researchers realized that this method was creating some obstacles to the interaction since the formal analytical procedures were unfamiliar for the local performers. Instead, a more informal conversation, without actual coding or use of CAQDAS, was tested for the final days of that trip.[19]

---

[18] Both are bowed string instruments and part of the larger family of two-stringed Asian fiddles.

[19] The interviews on the following days included encounters with the violinist Đặng Hoàng Linh and the guitarist Huỳnh Khải and were essential for supporting our early fieldwork in the Mekong delta (Östersjö & Nguyễn, 2022).

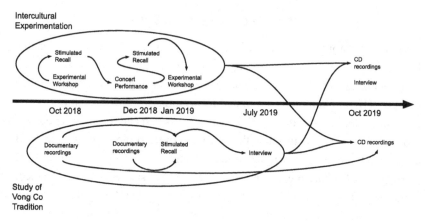

Figure 5 A timeline of the Musical Transformations research project

The fieldwork in Sài Gòn can be divided into three periods, each located in a different recording studio (see Figure 5). In the first and the last of the periods, in October–November 2018 and in October 2019 respectively, the group spent most waking hours busily at work in two major professional recording studios. But how do modern recording studios fit into urban areas defined by "tube housing" and "motorcycle culture" (Truong-Young & Hogan, 2020) in contemporary Vietnam? From the perspective of Sài Gòn streets, both recording studios used in this phase of the project blended well into their surroundings, among residences, tiny convenience shops, hair salons, and restaurants selling *phở* and *bánh mì*. At the same time, both studios were also negatively affected by traffic noise from a steady stream of motorbikes and trucks as well as construction projects, which led us to take breaks whenever excessive noise intruded into the recorded "takes." Local businesses were evidently accustomed to encountering foreigners leaving the studios for pauses in their recording sessions, and the musicians were warmly welcomed by local restaurants and cafes. In the evenings, the ensemble would gather at restaurants to reflect on what they had achieved each day, sometimes even adorned with performances of *Vọng Cổ* with voice and guitar, a social dimension, which contributed greatly to building both trust and empathy within the group.

Contrasting studio work with performances in restaurants brings to mind Bates's (2016) observation of how the design of recording studios in Istanbul may "create a vibe antithetical to certain forms of traditional music practice" (p. 147). However, in our understanding, even though *Vọng Cổ* is often heard in casual settings, the three Sài Gòn musicians were well acquainted with working in recording studios, which therefore can be regarded as a natural setting for their practice. In October–November 2018, the first working sessions with all musicians were carried out in the studio run by Huỳnh Tuấn, the *đàn kìm* player. On the first day, after a general presentation of the project, most of the time was spent giving space for the performers of the two groups to share recordings of earlier work and to discuss the different musical forms and projects that the participating musicians brought to the table. After this introduction, subsequent sessions were divided into two different strands that eventually shaped the design of the entire project: the documentation of traditional performance practices of *Vọng Cổ* on the one hand and experimentation with performance of this piece through intercultural collaboration on the other. The final sessions were dedicated to rehearsals for a performance scheduled at the Hanoi New Music Festival in December 2018. This would be the first public appearance of the two groups performing together in a concert at *L'Espace*, the concert hall of the *Institut Français* in Hà Nội.[20] We have previously noted how "meeting up in Hà Nội was a shift of scenery that had positive effects on the interaction between all performers. Now, The Six Tones were the host ensemble and would bring the other players around, to rehearsal and concert venues, cafes, and restaurants" (Nguyễn & Östersjö, pp. 192–93). The program was played to a full house, and it not only became the first milestone of our young collaboration but it was also contributed by increasing mutual respect and trust among the performers.

After the concert, the entire group returned to Sài Gòn to work in a studio at Vietnam National Institute of Culture and Art Studios (VICAS), a musicology research center. The work here can be divided into five somewhat overlapping phases. The first consisted of stimulated recall sessions based on review of video recordings from rehearsals in Hà Nội prior to the aforementioned concert. This was followed by a documentary recording session in which the entire group again performed the same structure as in the Hà Nội concert. Third, interviews with Môn, Ty, and Tuấn were carried out by Hebert and Nguyễn simultaneous to development of experimental collaborations among smaller constellations of performers, essentially whoever was not taking their turn being interviewed at that time in another room. Fourth, new recordings of solo and trio performances were made. Fifth, the last two days were devoted solely to stimulated recall, in which the three local master performers were presented with the complete set of recordings of *Vọng Cổ* produced thus far. This proceeded with a focus on comparison of recordings across the two sets of data from October and November, respectively, to discuss in detail which ones they prefer and why.

---

[20] In this performance Henrik Frisk was substituted by the Vietnamese composer and improviser Lương Huệ Trinh; Henrik Frisk reunited with the group in Sài Gòn for the sessions after this performance.

Method for the Study of Stimulated Recall in Musical Transformations

In order to assess the outcomes of the method development in the project, in January 2022, Frisk, Nguyễn, and Östersjö made a stimulated recall meta-study of a selection of videos drawn from sessions carried out in Sài Gòn in 2018–19. A schematic image of the analytical scenario in the meta-study can be seen in Figure 6. Largely remaining in the role of observers, Frisk, Nguyễn, and Östersjö reviewed each video recording of selected stimulated recall scenarios, still also drawing on their first-person understanding of having participated in each situation. Through a process of open coding (see Section 3), the analysis was structured and further annotated using HyperRESEARCH software. Hence, as suggested in Figure 6, they would negotiate an intersubjective understanding of each video, as part of the process of creating the codes and making annotations, which further outline their individual observations and interpretations of the situation.

The selection of clips for this meta-analysis was made by returning to video examples used in two book chapters: Stefan Östersjö's "The Vietnamese Guitar: Tradition and Experiment" (2022) and "Cultural Diplomacy and Transculturation through the History of the *Vọng Cổ* in Vietnam" by Nguyễn & Östersjö (2022). In these chapters, some of the findings from the Musical

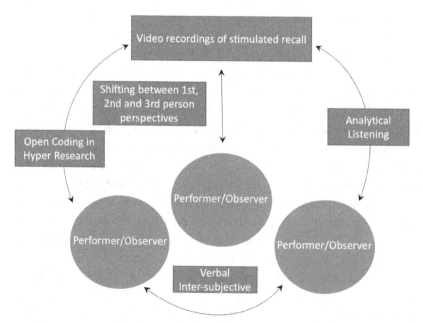

Figure 6 Schematic representation of the analytical design in the meta-study of data from Musical Transformations carried out in January 2022

Transformations project are discussed. The aim of the meta-analysis was twofold: first, to provide a further validation of the results presented in the aforementioned chapters, and second, to contribute to the present publication with a detailed analysis of how the stimulated recall was carried out and thereby to better understand the interpretative processes launched in these scenarios. For these purposes, while each selected clip in the book chapters is rather short and represents the main stimulated recall annotations discussed, here we included the entirety of the stimulated recall situation, from the start of the playback, with the surrounding comments and observations.

The representation of how the three researchers engaged with the stimuli suggests that, even if all three were engaged in the original situations as performers, they adopted a perspective as observers. This directed their focus of attention to the actions of all participants in the viewing and discussion during the stimulated recall situation, as captured on video. We will now outline the outcomes of the meta-analysis with a focus on two perspectives: first, how the participants engaged with the recordings of their performance, and second, how the verbal interactions between the participants in the recorded video contributed to a deepened understanding of the given situation, as well as to the artistic collaboration, as it was developing.

Stimulated Recall Scenarios in Musical Transformations

The entire group of performers met for the first time in Huỳnh Tuấn's studio on October 29, 2018. The morning was spent on sharing recordings from previous work of the two groups and on general conversations of how to go about the entire project. Thereafter, the afternoon was spent recording trio versions by Tuấn, Môn, and Ty of *Vọng Cổ* (henceforth referred to as "the three Sài Gòn musicians") with the aim of continuing the next day by recording their solo performances of the piece. In the afternoon of October 30, having completed this first round of recordings documenting *Vọng Cổ* in different historical forms, the entire group of performers formed different constellations to experiment with ways in which *Vọng Cổ* could be integrated in free improvisation with instruments and electronics, again, a form of music-making, which was entirely new to the three Sài Gòn musicians. The recordings made on the afternoon of October 30 were mixed by Stefan in the evening. The next morning, on October 31, the first stimulated recall session took place when the entire group of performers gathered again in Huỳnh Tuấn's studio, with everyone now gathered near the mixing board.

Building on the conclusions drawn from the previous interviews with guest musicians in the Mekong Delta (see the section "Timeline of the Project"), the design of these sessions was made with the main aim of making the three Sài Gòn musicians feel comfortable with the situation. One should also bear in mind that neither was particularly accustomed to talking about their music. Môn, perhaps being the exception, is a teacher in a school of theatre who also often teaches the guitar in other venues and appears more at ease with talking about his practice.[21] We felt that we managed pretty well in framing each stimulated recall session, which was carried out at the start of each working day in the studio, merely as an opportunity to listen back to the recordings from the preceding day and discuss their relative success and failure. It should be pointed out that the group of participants was significantly larger than in any session previously carried out by The Six Tones, as can also be seen in Figures 7–10. The design of the stimulated recall sessions in Musical Transformations was also immediately affected by the constraints and possibilities of both the particular space and the configuration of participants.

This entire procedure was repeated on each of the following days. Each day, after the recording sessions, Stefan[22] made draft mixes of the recordings, and selections of these recordings were played back to the entire group in the morning of the next day. Each stimulated recall session was recorded on audio and video, and these recordings have served as central data in the project and as the stimulus for the stimulated recall analysis in the meta-study presented in this section.

First Scenario: Seeking Shared Understanding

Huỳnh Tuấn studio is located in a dead-end alley in a small street in the otherwise busy 10th district in Sài Gòn. Together with some other artists, Huỳnh Tuấn rented the entire house, where they built several small studios. Tuấn's studio, on the third floor, is mainly dedicated to recording traditional music. Even though Huỳnh Tuấn created this studio to have a larger space than his previous home studio, this was indeed the narrowest space in which the group worked. Camera placement was difficult (in fact, even finding sufficient room for each performer when the entire group was to play was challenging enough), and this meant that not all participants were captured well on camera. The room was more akin to a corridor than a studio (a room shape not unusual in Vietnamese tube houses), which did contribute to a sense of intimacy and was further enhanced by the performers typically being seated close together on the floor. The Six Tones did our first experiments, performing with the three Sài

---

[21] In fact, the first meeting with Môn took place in the Mekong Delta with two members of the research team visiting teaching sessions in two different cities.

[22] We will in the following account of the analysis follow the Southeast Asian custom of addressing everyone by first name for simplicity.

Gòn musicians in this room, and consequently this was the first time they encountered the kind of experimental music that has become the trademark of The Six Tones.

After a brief introduction by Stefan, one of the pieces recorded the day before is played back from the start. At around 90 seconds into the piece, Thủy signals to stop the playback, as it reaches a point when a phrase in the *Vọng Cổ* is ending (see video example 3 in RC).[23] Môn and Thủy jointly agree it was a good location to pause, and Thủy turns to Ty, asking him to share his impressions of the music. She later turns to offer the same question to each of them. Three central codes in this clip are *seeking understanding, critical observation*, and *suggestion for improvement*,[23] and taken together they capture something of the atmosphere in this first scenario. Clearly, all three Sài Gòn musicians were confused by the music they heard and experienced a lack of aesthetic references, as expressed by Ty, who noted how "I wanted to listen to *Vọng Cổ* but I don't know what people are playing in here … sounds funny" (code: seeking understanding). Môn similarly explained, "I do not know what the taste of the Western audience is nowadays, but for us, with *Vọng Cổ*, we need to be in the right bar, in the right *Lái*, and play correctly" (critical observation). Tuấn was initially more positive, saying that he "finds it novel" but then made a similar reference to how the structure of *Vọng Cổ* is hard to identify in the performance, and he suggested that perhaps "there should be a sound or something to keep time, for the group to know where we are" (seeking understanding). All three had constructive suggestions related to how a clearer structure can be achieved. Ty suggested that the music could be divided into sections: "for instance, if we could play one *Lái* of *Vọng Cổ*, and on the next we play something different … If we play both at the same time, it will be hard to tell which *Lái* it is, which bar we are in, when we should stop" (suggestions for improvement). If much of Ty's account departed from a first-person perspective, at the end of this suggestion he adopted a third-person perspective, claiming that without a clearer structural organization, "the audience would be confused." Môn continued on the same thread, suggesting that

> [i]f we want to create something new in *Vọng Cổ*, which people would like to listen to, … in some parts we could combine different versions of *Vọng Cổ*, sometimes we play original, pure *Vọng Cổ*, play it well, sometimes we break the structure of the piece [...] but the main point is that if we do not want normal *Vọng Cổ*, we need to work with harmony (suggestions for improvement).

---

[23] When reference is made to codes in this chapter, these refer to the coding made in the meta-analysis and not to codes from the sessions recorded in Sài Gòn.

This was also an interesting moment, since Môn not only made critical observations of the experimental performance of *Vọng Cổ* but also turned to the present-day performance practice of this music as a reference, claiming that "until now, people listen to the same *Vọng Cổ*. It is good but can get boring. It lacks harmony." From this observation, Môn returned to the idea that arrangements that provide a different harmonic structure to *Vọng Cổ* could be attractive "both for Vietnamese and other audiences."

In our analysis, statements were coded either as mainly in first- or third-person perspective (see Figure 7). We found it interesting that the distribution of these codes was almost equal and that, in most cases, shifts between these perspectives within the same sentence or comment were a characteristic feature. We find that such shifts reflect the observation made by Laws (2019) of how, when we "speak subjectively of the subjective experience," we immediately find ourselves "outside: ejected from the moment, distanced from the dynamics of the subject position and no longer able to speak through it" (p. 17). At the same time, we observe how much of the verbal discourse is essentially inter-subjective and dialogical, as when Môn turned his critical observation to the musical culture of *Vọng Cổ*, very much as an invitation to a further dialogue around the potential for creating new arrangements of the piece using Western-style harmonization.

To summarize, according to our analysis of the first scenario, the session provided an example of initial doubts experienced by the three Sài Gòn musicians, but at the same time, we see how all three clearly wished to contribute to

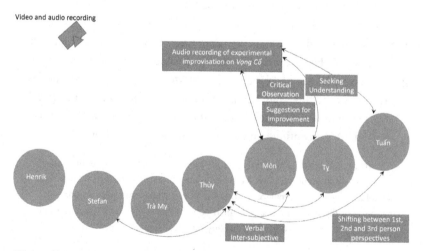

Figure 7 Schematic representation of the first stimulated recall scenario. See also video example 2 in RC

improving the work with the aim of creating music that could meet audiences both in Vietnam and abroad. Naturally, the atmosphere here was hesitant. It was a novel situation for the trio to be discussing music in this manner, let alone music that is significantly different from what they usually play, and, in particular, with musicians that traveled from another continent in order to collaborate in making music with them.

Second Scenario: An Experimental Performance

In the afternoon of October 31, Môn and Stefan recorded two pieces on electric and acoustic guitars combined with live electronics played by Henrik Frisk. These turned out to be the most radically different pieces so far, and the next morning, the first take was played back in its entirety. We coded eight moments of laughter among the musicians during this initial playback. Clearly, this quite experimental music, electronically manipulated to contain many sudden shifts of timbre, unexpected layers of sound, and an overall noisy character, was more provocative than any of the music from the stimulated recall session the day before. In the analysis of the conversation that followed, the same three codes, characteristic of the previous scenario, returned (see Figure 8). Tuấn was the first to comment, and he started out by noting that, for him, "it sounded like music for a scene in a play, rather than a composition" (code: seeking understanding). But from this observation he developed a further critique, stating that in any performance of *Vọng Cổ*, the ending should always be clearly articulated

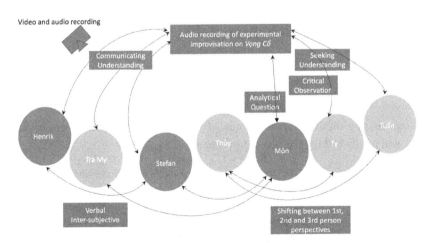

Figure 8 Schematic representation of the second stimulated recall scenario (light gray indicates that this musician did not perform in the current recording/ stimulus). See also video example 3 in RC

together. Indeed, not doing so is considered a big failure, and furthermore, the same holds for each structural downbeat in the framework of the song. Tuấn enforced his critique, aired on the previous day, that the performance did not match the aesthetic standards of the traditional musical practice that he knew. He noted how it simply "sounds better when all instruments end together" (code: critical observation). However, this scenario was different from the one the day before and had a much stronger dynamic in the dialogue between the performers. At this point, Trà My explained that her listening "is different," and that since she was familiar with Stefan's playing, she experienced "this music differently to you" (code: communicating understanding). While she agreed that there is a need to create clearer structures within which they can all interact, she found many parts of the experimental recording interesting and even that the playing offered new colors to *Vọng Cổ.*

This appeared to inspire Môn to pose a direct question to Stefan (or rather to ask Thủy to translate the question) of how Stefan finds it, performing on top of *Vọng Cổ* and breaking its structures. Môn also wanted Stefan to make a comparison to other performances (played in the first introductory day) in which experimental and traditional elements had been more smoothly integrated (the exact reference being a performance of *Tứ Đại Oán*, discussed in Section 3). Stefan responded that in these two performances he was "looking most of all for a sound, with the two guitars, that works, and the two guitars would be, all the time, in different musical spaces" (code: communicating understanding). But Stefan also explained that through all this, another goal was to challenge Môn's playing. Môn responded by noting how he himself didn't find many ways to interact with Stefan's playing: "I try, sometimes I stop, but then I do not find anything that can go along with what Stefan was doing" (code: critical observation). Thủy, also in her role as interpreter, summarized how this has to do with how the performers, who maintain the structures of *Vọng Cổ* in a performance, like Môn did in this piece, have less freedom to navigate within this "sound" and that perhaps he also had less tools to do so. Henrik, in a summarizing set of observations made by turning first to Stefan, then to Trà My, and finally to Môn, started out by stating:

> I agree with Stefan, it is obviously my intention too to try to find a sound that would work, and I think that was really successful, there were some openings in this, where there's, as you said My, an intention for a really unique sound, but it's really difficult for us to shape it. So this is, precisely as you were saying [turning to Môn], for you the challenge is to try to figure out how to play *Vọng Cổ* and then do this, but for us, the challenge is more on a sonical level, so that, in a way, it participates in pulling things apart rather than integrating them.

One may conclude that this scenario displayed a greater dynamic between the performers, brought friction between their respective traditions to the fore, and thereby may have indicated both challenges and possibilities in the collaboration (see video example 3 in RC).[24]

Based on the discussions (brought out in the stimulated recall sessions) regarding the possible advantages of creating clearer, and composed, structures, the group agreed that a large-scale form was to be created for the upcoming performance at the Hanoi New Music Festival. The remaining working days were dedicated to negotiating such a structure, which would respond to Ty's idea of creating a form derived from an oscillation between playing *Vọng Cổ* according to traditional performance practice and more experimental forms. Conceptually this may be compared to how a jazz performance may start off from a popular music form only to transform to what may seem to be a much more open musical expression and then, toward the end of the tune, go back to the original form again. In this way, the stimulated recall sessions on site contributed in a rather immediate manner to how the artistic work developed across this working week, and hereby also to the first artistic output, in the concert performance in Hà Nội.

Third Scenario: Returning to the Problem of Tonality

After the concert performance in Hà Nội, the largest city of northern Vietnam, the group reconvened in Sài Gòn from December 29, 2018. The sessions were carried out at VICAS, where one recording studio was located. Here, the group enjoyed a much larger space at their disposal with a small performance stage used both for lectures and concerts. A spacious and cool upstairs office affiliated with the musicology department was also made available for use. The stimulated recall sessions were set up in two different ways: when the entire group was involved, everyone sat in the audience seats of the performance space, and when the three Sài Gòn musicians (all three together or one at a time) became the focus of the stimulated recall session, they would be on the stage with the rest of the team seated in the audience. In many of the sessions, other researchers from VICAS also joined in with questions and comments. This combination of factors created a less-intimate atmosphere, but it was also more comfortable in longer sessions since there was so much more space allowing everyone to spread out. At VICAS, stimulated recall analysis became the main focus, which, during the final two days, was entirely devoted to the traditional versions of *Vọng Cổ* recorded so far in the project. But on the first working day, the very first stimulated recall session was carried out with the stimulus being

---

[24] All video examples are found in the following link: www.researchcatalogue.net/view/1301475/1302132.

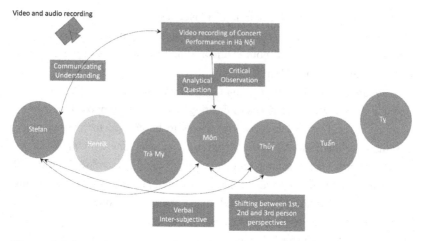

Figure 9 Schematic representation of the third stimulated recall scenario. See also video example 4 in RC

a longer recording of rehearsals from Hà Nội (see Figure 9). It was recorded on December 16 and 17, prior to the concert at Hanoi New Music Festival.

The entire team watched and listened to the playback of the entire piece as rehearsed for the Hà Nội performance in December 2018, and at the end, Môn was quick to pose a question regarding which version it had been (see video example 4 in RC).[25] When revisiting the video recording of the original stimulated recall session we were able to deepen our understanding of what had occurred. Môn noted that this was not one of the best takes and, typical of a musician's attention to their own performances, mentioned how his performance failed in *Vọng Cổ* 8 by mixing up phrases and playing the sixth phrase the double length. But, when he established an understanding of which version we were viewing (code: analytical question) and that, unfortunately, the better takes were lost due to a technical failure, he moved on to another more central question: whether the two contrasting trios (the Sài Gòn musicians and three members of The Six Tones) should play in the same key or not (code: analytical question)? Importantly, he described his listening experience as "a bit jarring (*nghịch tai*) to the ear," a phrase that would return one year later as a further development to the problem of tonality (code: critical observation). As a response to Môn's question, Stefan suggested that in fact, there were more convincing solutions for how the polytonal structure was performed in the concert, at the point to which Môn had referred. Furthermore, Stefan claimed

---

[25] All video examples are found in the following link: www.researchcatalogue.net/view/1301475/1302132.

that this rehearsal take did not give a proper representation of the artistic strategies, aimed at masking the entrance of a new and contrasting tonality, which the group had developed and tested in the rehearsals and the concert (code: communicating understanding).

If the second scenario was the most interactive, this excerpt has only two protagonists, Môn and Stefan. The dominating codes in this session were also different from the previous ones with "analytical question" and "critical observation" being the most recurrent. At the end of the session, Stefan suggested that in the documentary recording of this piece, the ensemble could first rehearse and further test these moments of contrasting tonalities. In our analysis of the third scenario based on the most recent stimulated recall, our overall impression was that the interaction had shifted, becoming more immediate, in a sense more technical and goal-oriented. While the more immediate interaction contributed to the artistic development, at the same time, it provided further evidence of how the music was perceived differently by the participating artists.

Fourth Scenario: Evaluation of Solo Performance

On the two last days at VICAS, all time was dedicated to stimulated recall sessions, in which the three Sài Gòn musicians listened and compared their performances of corresponding versions of *Vọng Cổ*, both as trios and solo performances. The relationship between the participating musicians again changed. Now the three Sài Gòn musicians had the (for them customary) role of master performers of *Vọng Cổ*, and all other participants assumed the role of observers. It should be noted that this shift in roles was reflected in the number of analytical questions, and third-person observations increased. To attain a manageable scope for this analysis, we will limit our focus to one key aspect of these sessions, Tuấn's evaluation of his solo playing, as also discussed by Östersjö and Nguyễn (2022).

Here, Tuấn was seated on stage with Thủy in the role of an interpreter, also taking questions from the "audience." In these sessions, the performers would normally have their instruments at hand and often clarify and further develop their observations through playing. The video material studied in the meta-analysis was a compilation of four segments from the same session, with some irrelevant bits taken out (see video example 5).

Characteristic of this scenario is the discussion of structure, both of compositional structure, in *Vọng Cổ* 8, an early version of the piece, which all three found difficult to master, and in the structuring of his solo playing in general. The sessions start out with David asking a question built on comparison of the initial improvisation, the *Rao*, which always opens a performance of *Vọng Cổ*.

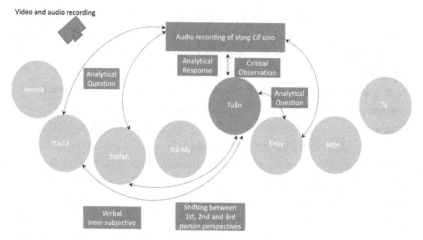

Figure 10 Schematic representation of the fourth stimulated recall scenario, in which only Tuấn had the role of performer, and all others took the role of observers. See also video example 5 in RC[26]

Prompted by this question, Tuấn continued to make comparison between two versions of the *Rao*, one introducing a performance of *Vọng Cổ* 8 and the other *Vọng Cổ* 16 (see Figure 10). He was not happy with the former and noted how "the music is not logically tied together. It is a little unconnected. The previous *Rao* had a better dynamic shape" (code: critical observation). Similarly, when listening to his performance of *Vọng Cổ* 8, he noted that "in general, *Vọng Cổ* 8 there are not many ways to design the phrase, because the Lái is so short" (code: critical observation). Stefan follows up on this statement by asking what performative strategies he employs to "do something good with *Vọng Cổ* 8." Tuấn expands on his first statement by noting how, "since the *Lái* is short, to be able to play it convincingly and with good flow … we need to play less figurations and more *Rung*, *Nhấn* (ornamentation), play it well so it sounds *mùi*" (code: analytical response).

The expression of *mùi* is the core aim in a performance of *Vọng Cổ* and is brought out as the central analytical feature in the book chapter discussing the Vietnamese guitar, building on stimulated recall interviews with Môn and his colleagues (see also Östersjö, 2022). The research team only started to grasp the nature of this feature of the performance practice across these days of stimulated recall at VICAS and returned to the subject again in the continued interview sessions with Môn in July the following year.

---

[26] All video examples are found in the following link: www.researchcatalogue.net/view/1301475/1302132.

On the Role of Questions

The four stimulated recall scenarios explained earlier are all drawn from the preparatory sessions in 2018–19, aimed at the final recording sessions for the double CD. In this concluding part of the section we will relate the observations mentioned earlier to findings in interviews made at the time of the recording sessions in October 2019. The recordings took place in the famous *Viết Tân* studio, one of the most productive recording studios in Sài Gòn, where a great number of hit recordings, in particular of *Nhạc vàng* (Yellow Music, a form of Southern Vietnamese pop music) had been mixed and mastered. Here, Torbjörn Samuelsson and Tomas Ferngren, two leading recording engineers from Sweden, brought a wealth of experience from decades of professional recording projects with an array of notable music ensembles. Still, the experimental music produced through this project was reportedly "unlike anything [they had] ever heard before." In our analysis of the stimulated recall scenarios, we found that the verbal interaction within the group had enabled an intersubjective negotiation of meaning. Starting out with the second scenario, we became interested in the role of questions in such interactions. In addition to mapping explicit questions, we also made observations of more overarching concerns, which we analyzed as implied questions. This related to how Östersjö and Nguyễn (2013) used the notion of the question in an expanded sense, also connecting it to how musical performance may take on the role of questions in musical dialogue. This led us to re-code the four scenarios, seeking to identify both implied and actual questions. In this final round of coding we identified both *how* questions and *why* questions and also, as we have seen in the earlier account, a number of *analytical* questions. For instance, in the second scenario, Môn asked Stefan how he experienced the performance, a question that led to a rather intricate discussion of the contrasting aesthetics that were at play in the collaboration. Further, we also coded a few instances of what we found to be *implied* questions, often in the form of observations of issues related to tonality or structure. What caught our interest in these questions is how they appear to articulate more overarching challenges and concerns in the project. We have seen how the "question of structure" in the initial improvisations in Tuấn's studio (scenarios 1 and 2) led to the creation of a fixed form for the first concert performance. Further, we can now see how the – sometimes explicit, sometimes implied – question of structure reoccurs in the fourth scenario but now is not related to the need to agree on ways to structure the experimental improvisations. Instead, it was when Tuấn compared his own playing in different versions of *Vọng Cổ* that critical observations were made of structural issues in his own performance, sometimes related also to how the form of *Vọng Cổ* 8 constrained his shaping of the *Lái*.

We have followed previously how Môn shares his listening to the different approaches to tonality, and to the modal structures of *Vọng Cổ*, which he encounters in the joint improvisations. In the stimulated recall session (third scenario) in which the entire group listens back to a rehearsal held before the concert in Hanoi, Môn uses the term *nghịch tai* to describe the jarring listening experience he had with reference to a section exploring polytonality. But a year later, in the concluding recording sessions, the three Sài Gòn musicians introduced the idea of playing *Vọng Cổ* traditionally but in three different keys simultaneously. In the final stimulated recall interview, Môn returns to the same Vietnamese phrase, when he describes how "when playing that version, my listening to their two instruments was inversed" (*nghịch tai*). We have already touched upon this as an example of how a musician's listening can be transformed, through encounters with musical Others, a perspective that Môn emphasizes by comparing his experience of listening in this trio performance to other performances within the project: "just like I have been experimenting and playing with other kinds of instruments" (Stimulated recall, October 2019).

Môn's shared listenings have contributed to deepening our understanding of the creative processes at play in intercultural collaboration. A similar contribution to new knowledge we find in the shared listening of Tuấn, when reflecting on his shaping of *Vọng Cổ* in his solos on the *dan kim*. Herein, a display of the constraints and possibilities in the structure of the different versions of *Vọng Cổ* are brought to light, but, importantly, Tuấn's final studio recordings also brought new perspectives by transcending the limitations he expressed in the stimulated recall session at VICAS. In a similar manner, Môn's stimulated recall of his performances of *Vọng Cổ* provided a foundational layer of knowledge, which laid the ground for a chapter on the Vietnamese guitar and its role in the development of *Vọng Cổ* and its performance practices (see also Östersjö, 2022). But the knowledge formation within the group of musicians goes further beyond these individual statements, observations, and reflections. The two book chapters presenting central results from Musical Transformations may also serve as examples of the double reflexivity, which Dietz (2011) advocates. As seen in the layers of qualitative analysis produced by The Six Tones, knowledge is produced through "an exchange between the two forms of aforementioned understandings: between the knowledge generated in the 'first order' by the 'experts' in their own point of view, and the ... knowledge generated in the 'second order' by the academic 'expert'" (Dietz, 2011, p. 14). We argue that the stimulated recall sessions have generated "a continuous and reciprocal critical and self-critical process" (Dietz, 2011, p. 14) between all participants along the lines of Dietz' proposal.

What emerged across this year of shared listening is first of all a mutual understanding, manifested in a particular way in the free improvisations made in the *Viết Tân* studio, which were performed with a striking ease and attentiveness. In a final interview, Ty made a comparison between the sessions in 2018 and the recording sessions, which were just finished, and he observed how "[l]ast year we tried, but we did not understand. This year we have a mutual understanding, really intertwined. It was really good. Even in the free improvisations we understand each other very well" (Ty, personal communication, October 16, 2019).

Taken together, we find that the use of stimulated recall appears to have contributed to both individual artistic development and the formation of a shared voice in the group. Additionally, it facilitated shared understandings of what is relevant situated knowledge in the development of *Vọng Cổ* and its performance practices.

Summary

The Musical Transformations project ultimately developed an approach to stimulated recall which was different from the methods of The Six Tones outlined in Section 3. We have seen already how the formal analytical procedures of coding and annotating the recording were replaced by a less-formal approach, sometimes built on interviewing and sometimes in the form of a joint conversation – involving a larger number of participants – more in the manner of a focus group interview. Similar to the stimulated recall methods discussed in Section 3, another central feature in Musical Transformations was how the process of shared listening within the group led to a transformed listening. As we have argued earlier, with reference to Dietz (2011), the stimulated recall analysis has allowed for a double reflexivity, and intersubjective knowledge production, which is a crucial factor in the attempt to decolonize music research methods.

5 Integrating Shared Listenings

Integration is a major theme that frequently appears in policy debates, whether it be the case of an arts institution that is seeking new ways of promoting social cohesion or a university that aims to diversify its offerings and make its education more relevant to a diverse population. While integration in this sense is one theme to be addressed in this section (with particular attention to the notions of social inclusion and decolonization), our primary focus will be on how the insights gained from the shared listenings approach in intercultural music ensembles may be *integrated* as public knowledge to be used by new generations of musicians. In a discussion of future prospects for world music ensembles in higher education, Robin Moore asked, "[S]hould the next frontier of our discipline be decolonizing performance programs?" (Moore, 2021, p. 229). We will begin here by considering the notions of bimusicality and transmusicality, the challenges of interdisciplinarity, and the characteristic features of transformed and decolonized listening. Further, we address later the use of stimulated recall as a decolonizing practice both for artistic development and in music research. We conclude with discussion of how our findings may be applied in both higher education and the creative spheres of artistry and scholarship.

Bimusicality and Transculturality

As Deschênes notes, upon reflecting on the methods of ethnomusicologists in the 1950s, Mantle Hood began "to realize at the time that being passive observer was not enough if they wanted to give an 'insider's view' of the music they were studying" (2018, p. 280). Deschênes expresses an appreciation for Hood's advocacy of *bimusicality* (Hood, 1960), which was certainly advanced for its time (nearly 60 years earlier), but Deschênes also emphasizes the notions of identity and embodiment in his advocacy of *transmusicality* as an additional concept to supplement bimusicality today. He sees bimusicality as emphasizing skills, while the notion of transmusicality could capture broader aspects of personal transformation as one deeply engages with a previously unfamiliar musical world:

> What the transmusical musician has to be able to do is to partially put aside (i.e., de-identify with) some of the musical training he has received from an early age (which can be extremely difficult to do, especially if it is considered a kind of musical and cultural truth), and must allow for another way of making sense of music in order to make it his own (i.e., re-identify). (Deschênes, 2018, p. 280)

However, Deschênes's view is not unlike that of Stephen Cottrell, who still argues that the notion of "bimusicality" remains relevant but could be expanded to mean "a component of self-conception, a way of both acquainting and aligning oneself with a combination of different performance aesthetics in order that an individual musician may discharge any one of them competently when called upon to do so" (Cottrell, 2007, p. 102). This widened definition allows Cottrell to include professional musicians, whose performances embrace more than one set of cultural codes within the range of bi-musical practices.

This extension allows us to make a series of observations regarding the role of bi-musicality in the practices of The Six Tones. First, when Nguyễn observes in the stimulated recall session in 2019 how what enabled the development of a shared voice in the group was in effect her individual development of a "new voice," this process could be described as an expression of transmusicality. Nguyễn's new voice certainly entailed developing such a repertoire of approaches to sound production on her instrument, in the manner that is also observed in the same set of stimulated recall sessions, noting her first use of "textural glissandos" in the concert performance at Atalante in Gothenburg (see also Section 3). For a rehabilitated notion of bi-musicality, or even transmusicality, there are particular ways it can be understood in the context of experimentation in intercultural music ensembles according to the arguments developed in this publication. First, the ensemble proceeds through a form of respectful "listening to the Other" (Östersjö, 2020), which invites embodied and participative recognition of divergent musical practices and their aesthetic systems. Secondly, as this mutual recognition is gained, the participating musicians aim to "translate" their own contributions in ways that will sensibly (and sensitively) join with the musical discourse of their collaborators, an approach that frequently entails experimentation with "intentionally representing significant aspects of one musical tradition through the techniques of another distinct tradition" (Hebert, 2018, p. 311). As the material is developed further, the ensemble gradually establishes its distinctive "voice" through a shared form of "extended cognition" as evidenced through its attainment of a fully participatory and inclusive approach to creation (Krueger, 2014).

Method Development at the Intersection between Disciplines

What then may the stimulated recall methods discussed in this Element contribute to the disciplines of artistic research and ethnomusicology? As we have seen earlier, there are many connecting points between the two, but what may be gained by fusing these approaches together through shared listening?

There are some notable examples outside the Musical Transformations project. For instance, in an ethnomusicological study of musical change in Tahiti, Geoffroy Colson aimed for similar research objectives. Colson (2014) sought "to comprehend processes through which pre-European contact music forms transform to 'become' contemporary music and to identify compositional processes employed in contemporary indigenous music making" (p. 7). The project design entailed a performing observer method, through which the "ethnomusicologist learns to play in order to obtain access to a more in-depth and intimate understanding of the aesthetics and creativity of the music" (p. 8). That project provided a rich overview of traditional practices and accounts of how heritage has evolved through transculturation. Through interviews, video recordings of performances, and analytical overviews, the project showed "how

Tahitian cultural specificity continues through a transcultural experience" (Colson, 2014, p. 19).

There are also general ways that ethnomusicology and artistic research may be compatible at the level of personal artistry. Artistic research at its fundamental core is all about documenting each step in the complex path for how an artist goes about improving and developing their artistry and offering the findings – and the artistic output – in a form from which other artists and pedagogues may learn. While most ethnomusicologists hesitate to declare most anything to be "universal" in the field of music, we can confidently assert that musicians in most any genre worldwide tend to constantly seek improvement in their personal artistry. Many have studied under great masters whom they respect and emulate, but there is often also an interest in obtaining even higher levels of mastery and of offering some unique contribution to one's tradition, perhaps even transforming it and taking the music in a new direction. Intercultural collaborations tend to be particularly "ear-opening" and inspiring for musicians who are facing any kind of "burn-out" or other such situation in which they lack new ideas for how to develop further as an artist, so it is reasonable to assume intercultural collaborations are likely to enrich musicians in the field of artistic research. Ethnomusicologists who are personally invested in attaining bimusicality, transmusicality, or even captivated by the details of performance interactions may thus see natural avenues for a fusion with artistic research approaches in their work.

Shared Listenings through Stimulated Recall

The usefulness of stimulated recall methods in music research lies in its ability to ground the research in the listening of participating musicians and researchers. Further, it is central to build these methods on listenings that are intersubjectively shared. When thinking of shared listenings as a feature of stimulated recall, it is not so much the experience of mutual understanding, of immediate connection, but rather the opposite that we find to be of central importance. Sharing of one's critique, any uncertainties, doubts or sense of concealment – as when Tuấn expresses his doubts about the qualities in the piece with two guitars and electronics – can be the beginning of a series of shared listenings.

In the exchanges between the performers, many different ways of hearing the same music were shared. As Thủy observed, Môn's difficulties when seeking to interact with Stefan's playing of a piece had to do with how he had less freedom to navigate within the "sound" created by Henrik and Stefan. She suggested that one reason was that Môn had to maintain the structures of *Vọng Cổ*, but also that he probably had less tools to engage with these novel sonorities. This stimulated recall session (second scenario in Section 4) pointed to a deeper understanding of the concepts and doubts that had already been put on the table. But, as we already concluded in Section 4, the discussion of the role of tonality and structure became essential for the further artistic development and also for a deepened understanding of the cultural codes of the *Vọng Cổ* tradition.

Another example can be drawn from the final interview with Tuấn, in October 2019, wherein he made some reflections on the effects the project had on his listening. He first observed how the high-quality recordings of each performance, and the repeated joint listening back to these, had been a central factor in how he had developed new aspects to his playing since the project started. Tuấn described how this approach was one reason why the final CD recordings came together as they did, further reflecting on how his experience of experimenting with *Vọng Cổ* with The Six Tones has changed over time. Tuấn described how he "feels more integrated in the group now." The concerns Tuấn expressed early in the process, along with a wish for clearer structures to help keep the time, transformed into a rather different description:

> I feel deep inside that it makes my playing very free. Since your playing is so free, I can also play anything. There is no constraining composition or time-frame, it is free. Therefore I feel very free and comfortable. (Huỳnh Tuấn, Interview, October 16, 2019)

In the study of intercultural collaboration, stimulated recall offers access to processes that would otherwise be deeply concealed in the embodiment of each participant. In order to bring transformational individual artistic experience to light, the shared listenings approach to stimulated recall has proven to be an important vehicle in the Musical Transformations project, as well as in the earlier work of The Six Tones.

Transformed Listening to the Other

Across the fourth section, we have followed how Môn shares his listening to the different approaches to tonality and to the modal structures of *Vọng Cổ*, which he encounters in the joint improvisations. In the stimulated recall session (third scenario) in which the entire group listens back to a rehearsal held before the concert performance in Hanoi, Môn uses the term *nghịch tai* to describe the jarring listening experience he had, with reference to a section exploring polytonality. But a year later, in the concluding recording sessions, the three Sài Gòn musicians introduced the idea of playing *Vọng Cổ* traditionally but in three different keys simultaneously. In the final stimulated recall interview, Môn returns to the same Vietnamese phrase, when he describes how "when playing that version, my listening to their two instruments was inversed" (*nghịch tai*). We have already touched upon this as an example of how a musician's listening can be transformed, through encounters with musical Others, a perspective that Môn emphasizes by comparing his experience of listening in this trio performance to other performances within the project: "just like I have been experimenting and playing with other kinds of instruments" (Stimulated recall, October 2019).

Similarly, in Section 3, we have seen how the stimulated recall analysis, and in particular, through the repeated re-coding of the documentation, has brought forth an understanding of how it was necessary for Thủy to develop a new voice in order to fully contribute in the improvised interaction. We argue that similar processes of transformed listening have shaped the artistic development of each member of the group. This eventually generated a shared voice, which sometimes has been characterized by a friction between individual expressions, and sometimes by blending in, through integrated listening. Nguyễn and Östersjö (2019) find

> these two contrasting approaches to be equally strong expressions of an ethical approach to the musical other. Hospitality expressed through the principle of blending may be understood as attentive listening based on adaptation. Blending emerges from a search for sameness. The discursive heterogeneous voice instead builds on the creation of a space for co-existence and a celebration of difference. (p. 253)

In retrospect, the analytical approach, taken in the first stimulated recall sessions in 2009, of analyzing the interaction in the group as different modes of listening appears to have captured a key element in the artistic development as it eventually unfolded. In the final analysis, it is through transformed listening that the development of a shared voice in the group, and further the potential for shared listenings with other artists, became possible.

Implications for a Decolonized Collaborative Musical Practice

As mentioned in the first section, the rationale for decolonizing systems of musical thinking is to enable more equitable approaches to musical practices. This must entail a questioning of dominant Western structures, such as conventional music theory and hegemonic musical idioms, in an effort to create space for different modes of operation. As evidenced in the examples of intercultural collaboration in Sections 3 and 4, the disruptive effect that new knowledge can have on performance practice may eventually pave the way for new possibilities, new expressions, and entirely new modes of listening.

With regard to artistic development and research, a particular strength of stimulated recall method in this context is how the process of sharing listening within a group of collaborating musicians may lead to a transformed listening that informs the musical interaction. Further, concerning development of decolonized music research methods, stimulated recall analysis can be a tool for creating a "double reflexivity" (Dietz, 2011) as evidenced through the modes of intersubjective knowledge production explored in the present publication. Hereby, the processes of making observations and analysis are distributed between "first" and "second order" and between insider and outsider participants. Following Dietz, at this stage "any possible contradiction that results from the exchange of both perspectives should be integrated by the ethnographer in the same process of investigation, which will oscillate dialectically between identification and distancing, between grades of complete agreement and grades of analytical reflection" (Dietz, 2011, p. 14). Ultimately, we argue that stimulated recall offers methods for developing decolonized listening practices, both in the contexts of artistic research and ethnomusicology, and that they hold a promise to contribute to decolonizing these music practices.

Methodological Approaches and Technological Mediation

A basic structural factor in the stimulated recall sessions of The Six Tones was that, with few exceptions, the coding was made from video documentation. However, as can be seen in the analysis presented in Section 3, the representation of the interaction was analyzed as sound, through different modes of listening, with very little reference to visual interaction.

The approach to documentation was somewhat different in Musical Transformations. The decision to hold all working sessions in recording studios signaled a focus on producing high-quality audio documentation. Our determination to produce high-quality audio recordings was a motivating factor for the Sài Gòn musicians and also, as expressed by Tuấn, a component in their artistic development through the project.

In the meta-analysis of the stimulated recall sessions in Musical Transformations (see Figure 6, in Section 4) the interaction was coded to a greater extent from the video, rather than from the audio. Although the video was recorded consistently with only one camera, it was sufficient for producing the analysis. However, it should be pointed out that in many other situations, an approach using multiple cameras is often necessary. The analytical focus in both projects was on the musicians' listening, and therefore the documentation was designed to capture the music interaction in high resolution while the role of the video was to provide context to the flow of events.[27]

It is also possible to develop a stimulated recall design that emphasizes the advantages of shifting between different modalities (for an example of such approaches see Stefansdottir and Östersjö 2022). This brings us back to the discussion of connection and detachment, and their complementary qualities, suggesting for instance the possibility to create situations that engender "detachment in order to see all the relevant interconnections" (Bresler, 2009, p. 12). Going back to Vermersch's idea (1999) of how the intentionality of the technology affects the possibility to access lived experience (through reflection and metareflection), it is clear how technology-enhanced stimulated recall enables unique insights into musicianship. When reflecting on an event, the subject again experiences living through another instance of lived experience, which, in a stimulated recall scenario, is also immediately affected by the intentionality of the technology. This relation can be analyzed as a composite intentionality, which brings together the human and the nonhuman intentionalities.

The quality of audio recordings, the nature of the video documentation (e.g., with single or multiple angles), the general resolution of the data, the possibility of abstract representations (spectrograms and other analytical tools), other multimedia representations, and the playback situation (audio and video facilities) influence and configure the technological intentionality, which together with the subject's intentionality constructs a composite intentionality. This all suggests that the design of stimulated recall analysis must always take into account the particular possibilities and constraints related to the composite intentionality of human and technology. Returning then to Taylor's (1985) question cited in Section 2, whether it is indeed possible "to recall a thought in its original state" (p. 36), we argue that stimulated recall analysis entails more than merely the possibility for a subject to relive an original situation. Rather, it offers a rich set of possibilities for connection and detachment with the aim of making the familiar strange and allowing for heightened perception.

Implications of Decolonization for Higher Music Education

Across recent years there has been much discussion of how higher education music programs might be reformed and rejuvenated through efforts to broaden the curriculum to include more diverse forms of music as well as updated use of

---

[27] However, in other projects with The Six Tones, video analysis has been at the center of focus, as can be seen in projects like Inside/Outside (Nguyễn, 2019; Nguyễn & Östersjö, 2020) and Go to Hell (Östersjö, 2016).

technologies (Moore, 2017; Sarath, Myers, & Campbell, 2016). Furthermore, there is also a strong movement toward establishing dialogical forms of teaching beyond the traditional master-apprentice model (Jørgensen, 2014). All three of these areas – musical diversity, technological applications, and democratic leadership models – are fields in which our findings from this Element are relevant.

In major universities in the United States that support ethnomusicology PhD programs – such as the University of Texas, the University of California, Los Angeles, and the Wesleyan University – a great variety of "world music" ensembles can be found, from Indonesian gamelan, to Chinese music, North Indian music, mariachi bands, salsa bands, and so on (Solís, 2004). As suggested in a recent publication, "Creating World Music" is one reasonable sphere of activity to pursue in the context of a world music ensemble in higher education (Coppola, Hebert, & Campbell, 2021), with activities that entail not only sustaining a tradition through performance that aims for some version of "authenticity" toward heritage but even creating new music. However, what we are suggesting here is that this can be reasonably supported not only in alignment with the aesthetics of a specific tradition but also within cross-cultural experimentations. In other words, methods from *both* ethnomusicology and artistic research can be valuable in this field.

Moore (2021) recently claimed that "[i]nstitutions resist change, but the time is right to offer a new vision of performance training. And in that effort ethnomusicology is poised to play a central role" (p. 234), a statement that confirms a current trend and indicates that in the renewal of Higher Music Education (HME) curricula, methods from both artistic research (REACT, 2021) and ethnomusicology hold great potential. The examples discussed in this Element also contribute to this field with some alternative approaches that may be applicable in HME. Indeed, offering space for experimental intercultural ensembles, like The Six Tones, would likely be considered a radical gesture in most conservatoire settings and require some high-tech infrastructure to be implemented – including high bandwidth internet, quality video cameras, microphones, and mixing equipment – so rehearsals and performances can be planned as live telematic collaborations with other such ensembles in other parts of the world. What can be gained through such a bold step is direct access to "culture bearers," who can open students' ears to the vast diversity of musical expressions that exist worldwide, rather than being limited to what may be available in their local community. Online collaborations also tend to eventually lead to face-to-face collaborations when that becomes feasible. Telematic performance in this way can become a new form of internationalization and an innovative way of bringing cultural diversity into higher education.

The recent COVID-19 pandemic has especially shown how online collaborations of this kind can be useful, but they are much more effective when carefully planned than when hastily improvised due to the unexpected constraints of a pandemic lockdown.

We argue that the benefits of stimulated recall, and the intersubjective knowledge formation through a double reflexivity, which it offers, entail a method which may successfully be implemented in performance training in HME. Since it is a method grounded in listening, it offers efficient techniques, which can be readily integrated into teaching. The perspectives discussed earlier, regarding the many opportunities for designing specific interactions with technology, are equally pertinent for educational contexts.

Along the same lines, the field of artistic research has developed methods for integrating artistic development with reflexive and analytical strategies, but the implementation of such procedures in HME is still in its early stages. This also fits with Robin Moore's recent advocacy for a "greater centrality of performance as a component of ethnomusicological training" (Moore, 2021, p. 219), which is partly based on the realization that "[m]any ethnomusicologists involved in performance have found that playing music affords insights into the arts that complement academic inquiry; the two realms need not be conceived as distinct, but as mutually reinforcing" (p. 229).

Applications to Artistry and Scholarship

In the introductory section we described how this Element will appeal to rather different kinds of prospective readers for very different reasons. This includes *traditional music performers* from anywhere who seek to develop successful intercultural collaborations, as well as *music researchers* (such as ethnomusicologists, music psychologists, and those engaged in "artistic research") who seek to better understand musical practices; *contemporary composers and performers of experimental art music* (including music with electro-acoustic, avant-garde, and improvisational elements) who seek new ways of expanding their art form, and finally, specialists in *Vietnamese music* who are curious to consider new intercultural developments in this field. It is useful now to consider what are some of the main points we have reached that will be valuable to each kind of reader.

Our description of the use of stimulated recall methods for an effective and democratic artistic development in The Six Tones offers a useful approach that may also be applicable to musicians in many other contexts who seek practical and effective methods for collaboration. What we have shown through our depiction of the approach taken by The Six Tones is likely to work well in other settings in which musicians from vastly different traditions seek to develop new forms of collaborative artistry.

Ethnomusicologists and other music researchers may find that our methods enable new ways of probing more deeply into diverse forms of traditional musical aesthetics. By using technologies to systematically present traditional musicians with different versions of their own performances and asking them to select the better one while fully explaining the reasoning for their preferences, it is possible for researchers to obtain precise and tangible insights that might not otherwise be possible with such complex phenomena. Further, we argue that stimulated recall methods may enable a double reflexivity in the way such methodological approaches are discussed by Dietz (2011), a decolonizing approach, which we believe may be useful in ethnomusicological inquiry.

We are confident that the approaches taken here will also be of great interest to some contemporary composers and experimental art music performers, particularly considering the collaborative approaches and the search for inter-actions that embrace a dynamic between sameness and difference. Similar approaches could be taken in other contexts to creatively develop new sounds that would enrich the increasingly global field of experimental art music. We see many indications that this is a promising direction for the future of art music, which has often in the past been accused of having elitist and ethnocentric connotations (Utz, 2021). By cooperating with musicians from entirely different traditions on an equal footing that shows respect for their divergent orientations, we find that composers are likely to be challenged and stimulated in new ways, suggesting new avenues for "global art music" (Utz, 2021, p. 38). By cooperating with researchers in such projects, composers are able to shape their own narratives. Particularly when the composers themselves come from Asia, through such an approach, "the composers in question are no longer the silent Other, but rather, interlocutor" (Rao, 2014, p. 236), thereby exercising agency in the creation of new musical forms.

Specialists in Vietnamese music will also confirm that through this project we have developed new knowledge, which is of interest in a variety of ways. First, by conducting a series of professional recording sessions with recognized masters of traditional music, which has not previously been preserved in high-quality digital recordings, the project has contributed to the sustainability of unique musical heritage from the Mekong delta. The experimental collaborations through this project have emerged from an active engagement in the communities for experimental music in the country. Their practice has contributed to stimulating a new generation of Vietnamese musicians, interested in developing effective fusions of Vietnamese traditional music elements with Western art music techniques, as has been seen in the prominent work of

Asian composers from other countries, such as Toru Takemitsu from Japan, Isang Yun from Korea, and Tan Dun from China, who are now known worldwide (Lau, 2017; Lee, 2021). In our view, music scholars should encourage both kinds of work, that of sustaining traditional heritage and of careful experimentation with possible fusions that might reinvigorate the music field in various ways. Experimental fusions can develop in an array of configurations, merging different local genres with styles that include not only art music but also popular music (Norton, 2013; Ó Briain, 2021) and even jazz (Tan-Tangbau & Minh, 2021). We should note that when heritage is already successfully sustained, new forms can also be developed by "inventing musical techniques that stretch the boundaries of what is traditionally 'correct'. Only a musical culture very secure with itself could tolerate such experimentation " (Tenzer, 1991, p. 25). Music experimentation can thus proceed with the objectives of both developing something new for its own sake and presenting valued elements of the traditional heritage in an approachable way that might also, in time, attract new audiences to earlier forms.

Concluding Remarks

From the start of this Element, we acknowledged the search for "fragments of ourselves" that many non-European peoples have struggled to reassemble and *integrate* as part of the postcolonial condition (Smith, 2012). We therefore identified the need for decolonized approaches in both music artistry and scholarship and reflected on what this could mean in the context of intercultural and experimental ensembles. In our attempts to conduct music research beyond the "white racial frame" (Ewell, 2021), we have aimed to show how intersubjective knowledge formation can be developed through an approach of shared listening, mutual understanding, and stimulated recall methods. We thereby aspire to make a contribution to "musicology's gradual move towards decolonizing its epistemic and institutional structure" (Yamauchi, 2019, p. 333), while also hoping that the artistic practices and the research presented in the publication will contribute more widely to the development of more inclusive and sustainable music cultures.

References

Adorno, T. W. (1989). *Introduction to the Sociology of Music*. New York: Continuum.

Agawu, K. (2003). *Representing African Music: Postcolonial Notes, Queries, Positions*. New York: Routledge.

Allen, J. S., & Jobson, R. C. (2016). The decolonizing generation: (Race and) theory in anthropology since the eighties. *Current Anthropology*, 57(2), 129–48. https://doi.org/10.1086/685502.

Alvesson, M., & Sköldberg, K. (2017). *Reflexive Methodology: New Vistas for Qualitative Research*. Thousand Oaks, CA: Sage.

Arlander, A. (2008). Finding your way through the woods - Experiences of artistic research. *Nordic Theatre Studies*, **20, 28–41**.

Bailey, D. (1992). *Improvisation: Its Nature and Practice in Music*. Cambridge, MA: Da Capo Press.

Bastien, D. T. (2022). Interview with David G. Hebert, January 8, 17:00 CET.

Bastien, D. T., & Hostager, T. J. (1988). Jazz as a process of organizational innovation. *Communication Research*, 15(5), 582–602.

Bastien, D. T., & Hostager, T. J. (1992). Cooperation as communicative accomplishment: A symbolic interaction analysis of an improvised jazz concert. *Communication Studies*, 43(2), 92–104.

Bastien, D. T., & Hostager, T. J. (1996). On cooperation: A replication of an experiment in jazz and cooperation. *Comportamento Organizacional e Gestao*, 2(1), 33–46.

Becker, J. (2010). Exploring the habitus of listening: Anthropological perspectives. In P. N. Juslin & J. A. Sloboda, eds., *Handbook of Music and Emotion: Theory, Research, Applications*. Oxford: Oxford University Press, pp. 127–57.

Bell, A. P. (2013). Oblivious trailblazers: Case studies of the role of recording technology in the music-making processes of amateur home studio users (Order No. 3553941). ProQuest One Academic. https://search.proquest.com/docview/1316589551?accountid=8579.

Benaquisto, L. (2008). Open coding. In L. Given ed., *The SAGE encyclopedia of qualitative research methods*. Thousand Oaks: SAGE Publications, Inc, pp. 581–82.

Bernasconi, R. (2020). Frantz Fanon's Engagement with Phenomenology: Unlocking the Temporal Architecture of Black Skin, White Masks. *Research in Phenomenology* **50 (3)**, **386–406**. doi:10.1163/15691640-12341458.

Bhambra, G. K., Gebrial, D., & Nisancioglu, K., eds., (2018). *Decolonising the University*. London: Pluto Press.

Biggs, M. & Karlsson, H. (eds.) (2011). *The Routledge Companion to Research in the Arts*. Routledge.

Blain, M. & Minors, H. J. eds. (2020). *Artistic Research in Performance through Collaboration*. Basingstoke: Palgrave.

Bloom, B. S. (1953). Thought processes in lectures and discussions. *The Journal of General Education*, 7(3), 160–69.

Bresler, L. (2009). Research education shaped by musical sensibilities. *British Journal of Music Education*, 26(1), 7–25. https://doi.org/10.1017/S0265051 708008243.

Cannon, A. (2012). Virtually audible in diaspora: The transnational negotiation of Vietnamese traditional music. *Journal of Vietnamese Studies*, 7(3), 122–56.

Chávez, L., & Skelchy, R. P. (2019). Decolonization for ethnomusicology and music studies in higher education. *Action, Criticism, and Theory for Music Education*, 18(3), 115–43.

Chen, S.-L. S. (1995). Carl Couch: Bridging sociology and communication. *Symbolic Interaction*, 3(18), 323–39. www.jstor.org/stable/10.1525/si.1995.18.3.323.

Cobussen, M., & Nielsen, N. (2012). *Music and Ethics*. Farnham: Ashgate.

Colombo, M., Irvine, E., & Stapleton, M., eds., (2019). *Andy Clark and His Critics*. New York: Oxford University Press.

Colson, G. (2014). A fresh approach to transculturation in contemporary music in Tahiti. *Eras*, 16(1), 1–22.

Connell, R. (2018). Decolonizing sociology. *Contemporary Sociology*, 47(4), 399–407.

Coppola, W. J., Hebert, D. G., & Campbell, P. S. (2021). *World Music Pedagogy, VII: Teaching World Music in Higher Education*. New York: Routledge.

Cottrell, S. (2007). Local bimusicality among London's freelance musicians. *Ethnomusicology*, 51, 85–105.

Cumming, N. (2000). *The Sonic Self: Musical Subjectivities and Signification*. Bloomington: Indiana University Press.

Davies, S. (2011). *Musical Understandings and Other Essays in the Philosophy of Music*. Oxford: Oxford University Press.

De Souza, J. (2017). *Music at Hand: Instruments, Bodies, and Cognition*. New York: Oxford University Press.

Deschênes, B. (2018). Bi-musicality or transmusicality: The viewpoint of a non-Japanese shakuhachi player. *International Review of the Aesthetics and Sociology of Music*, 49(2), 275–94.

DeWald, E. (2012). Taking to the waves: Vietnamese society around the radio in the 1930s. *Modern Asian Studies*, 46(1), 143–65.

Dietz, D. (2011). Towards a doubly reflexive ethnography: A proposal from the anthropology of interculturality. *AIBR: Revista de Antropología Iberoamericana*, 6(1), 3–26. https://doi.org/10.11156/aibr.060102e.

Elo, M. & M. Luoto, M., eds., (2018). *Figures of Touch: Sense, Technics, Body*. The Academy of Fine Arts at the University of the Arts Helsinki.

Emmerson, S. (2006). Appropriation, exchange, understanding. Paper presented at the EMS Conference, Beijing. Available at http://www.ems-network.org/spip.php?article292.

Erickson, F. (2011). Uses of video in social research: A brief history. *International Journal of Social Research Methodology*, 14(3), 179–89. https://doi.org/10.1080/13645579.2011.563615.

Ewell, P. (2021). Music theory's white racial frame. *Music Theory Spectrum*, 43(2), 324–29. https://doi.org/10.30535/mto.26.2.4.

Ewell, P. (2020). Music Theory and the White Racial Frame. *MTO*. 26(2), doi: 10.30535/mto.26.2.4.

Falthin, A. (2015). *Meningserbjudanden och val*. Stockholm: Royal Academy of Music.

Fleck, L. (1981). *Genesis and Development of a Scientific Fact* (T. J. Trenn & R. K. Merton, Eds.; F. Bradley & T. J. Trenn, Trans.). Chicago: University of Chicago Press (original work published in German in 1935).

Foucault, M. (1997). *The Essential Works of Michel Foucault, 1954-1984*. New York: New Press.

Frisk, H. (2013). The (un)necessary self. In H. Frisk & S. Östersjö, eds., *(re) thinking Improvisation: Artistic Explorations and Conceptual Writing*. Malmö: Malmö Academy of Music, pp. 143–56.

Frisk, H. (2014). Improvisation and the self: To listen to the other. In F. Schroeder & M. Ó hAodha, eds., *Soundweaving: Writings on Improvisation*. Newcastle: Cambridge Scholars, pp. 153–69.

Frisk, H., & Karlsson, H. (2010). Time and interaction: Research through non-visual arts and media. In M. Biggs & H. Karlsson, eds., *The Routledge Companion to Research in the Arts*. New York: Routledge, pp. 272–92.

Frisk, H., & Östersjö, S. (2006). Negotiating the musical work: An empirical study. Paper presented at International Computer Music Conference, ICMC 2006, New Orleans, United States, pp. 242–49.

Frisk, H., & Östersjö, S., eds. (2013). *(re)thinking Improvisation: Artistic Explorations and Conceptual Writing*. Malmö: Malmö Academy of Music

Gallese, V. (2014). Bodily selves in relation: embodied simulation as second-person perspective on intersubjectivity. *Philosophical Transactions of the Royal Society*, 369, 20130177.

Gazdag, E., Nagy, J., & Szivak, J. (2019). "I spy with my little eyes . . .": The use of video stimulated recall methodology in teacher training – the exploration of aims, goals and methodological characteristics of VSR methodology through systematic literature review. *International Journal of Educational Research*, 95, 60–75.

Gorton, D., & Östersjö, S. (2019). Austerity measures I: Performing the discursive voice. In C. Laws, W. Brooks, D. Gorton et al. eds., *Voices, Bodies, Practices*. Orpheus Institute Series. Leuven: Leuven University Press, pp. 29–79.

Hebert, D. G. (2018). Cultural translation and musical innovation: A theoretical model with examples from Japan. In D. G. Hebert, ed., *International Perspectives on Translation, Education and Innovation in Japanese and Korean Societies*. New York: Springer, pp. 309–31. https://doi.org/10.1007/978-3-319-68434-5_20.

Hebert, D. G. (2021). Editorial introduction: Global competence, decolonization, and Asian educational philosophies. *Nordic Journal of Comparative and International Education (NJCIE)*, **5(2)**, **1–7**. https://doi.org/10.7577/njcie.4158.

Hebert, D. G. (2022). Ethnomusicology as a resource for cultural diplomacy. In D. G. Hebert & J. McCollum, eds., *Ethnomusicology and Cultural Diplomacy*. Lanham, MD: Lexington Books, pp. 3–19.

Hebert, D. G. (ed.), (2023). *Comparative and Decolonial Studies in Philosophy of Education*. Cham: Springer.

Hebert, D. G. & J. McCollum. (2014). Philosophy of history and theory in historical ethnomusicology. In D. G. Hebert & J. McCollum, eds., *Theory and Method in Historical Ethnomusicology*, Lanham, MD: Lexington Books, pp. 85–147.

Heikinheimo, T. (2009). *Intensity of Interaction in Instrumental Music Lessons*. Sibelius Academy. Music Education Department. Doctoral dissertation.

Hood, M. (1960). The challenge of "bi-musicality." *Ethnomusicology*, 4(2), 55–59.

Hood, M. (1971). *The Ethnomusicologist*. New York: McGraw-Hill

Hultberg, C. (2005). Practitioners and researchers in cooperation – method development for qualitative practice-related studies, *Music Education Research*, 7(2), 211–24. https://doi.org/10.1080/14613800500169449.

Huỳnh, C. T. (2016) Th.nh Tựu bản Vọng Cổ & những đ.ng g.p của nghệ sỹ nh.n d.n Viễn Ch.u. *Xưa Nay*, 476, 62–65.

Ihde, D. (2007). *Listening and Voice: Phenomenologies of Sound*. 2nd ed. Albany: State University of New York Press.

Johnson-Laird, P. N. (2002). How Jazz musicians improvise. *Music Perception*, 19(3), 415–42.

Jørgensen, H. (2014). Western classical music studies in universities and conservatoires. In I. Papageorgi & Graham F. Welch, eds., *Advanced Musical Performance: Investigations in Higher Education Learning*. Farnham: Ashgate, pp. 3–20.

Kagan, N., & Krathwohl, D. (1967). *Studies in Human Interaction: Interpersonal Process Recall Stimulated by Videotape*. East Lansing: Michigan State University, College of Education, Educational Publication Services.

Kempe, A.-L., & West, T. (2022). Interview with David G. Hebert, January 12, 10:00 CET.

Kiều, T. (1997). C.y D.n Ghita Ph.m L.m. In K. Schwaen, G. Jähnichen, and J. Wischermann (eds.), Schriften und Dokumente zur Politik, Wirtschaft und Kultur Vietnams 9. Berlin: Deutsch-Vietnamesische Gesellschaft, pp. 1–91.

Koch, F. (2021). Transculturation and contemporary artistic collaboration: Pushing the boundaries of histories, epistemologies, and ethics: Introduction. *The Journal of Transcultural Studies*, 11(2), 1–18. https://doi.org/10.17885/heiup.jts.2020.2.24287.

Kress, G. Selander, S., Säljö, J., & Wulf, C., eds., (2021). *Learning as Social Practice: Beyond Education as an Individual Enterprise*. New York: Routledge.

Kress, G., & van Leeuwen, T. (2001). *Multimodal Discourse: The Modes and Media of Contemporary Communication*. London: Arnold.

Krueger, J. (2014). Affordances and the musically extended mind. *Frontiers in Psychology*, 4, 1003. https://doi.org/10.3389/fpsyg.2013.01003.

Lau, F. (2017). Musical modernism in Asia. In S. Ross & A. C. Lindgren, eds., *The Modernist World*. New York: Routledge, pp. 62–69.

Laws, C. (2019). Introduction. In C. Laws, W. Brooks, D. Gorton et al. eds., *Voices, Bodies, Practices: Performing Musical Subjectivities*. Orpheus Institute Series. Leuven: Leuven University Press, pp. 235–94.

Lê, T. H. (2003). Huế and Tài Tử music of Viet Nam: The concept of music and social organisation of musicians. *ePapyrus. Australian Asia Foundation*. https://sonicjournal.files.wordpress.com/2014/01/hueandtaitumusic.pdf.

Lee, T. S., ed., (2021). *Routledge Handbook of Asian Music: Cultural Intersections*. New York: Routledge.

Levinas, E. (1979). Totality and Infinity: An Essay on Exteriority. The Hague: Martinus Nijhoff. First published 1961 as Totalité et infini: Essai dur l'extériorité (The Hague: Martinus Nijhoff).

Lewis, G. (2021). New music decolonization in eight difficult steps. *Outernational*, 14, n.p. www.van-outernational.com/lewis-en/.

Mackinlay, E. (2015). Decolonization and applied ethnomusicology: "Storying" the personal-political-possible in our work. In S. Pettan & J. T. Titon, eds., *The Oxford Handbook of Applied Ethnomusicology*. New York: Oxford University Press, pp. 379–97.

Mahendran, D. (2007). The facticity of blackness. *Human Architecture: Journal of the Sociology of Self-Knowledge*, 5, 191–203.

Matta, C. (2019). Qualitative research methods and evidential reasoning. *Philosophy of the Social Sciences*, 49(5), 385–412. https://doi.org/10.1177/0048393119862858.

Mbembe, A. J. (2016). Decolonizing the university: New directions. *Arts & Humanities in Higher Education*, 15(1), 29–45.

McCollum, J., & Hebert, D. G., eds., (2014). *Theory and Method in Historical Ethnomusicology*. Lanham, MD: Lexington Books.

McKerrell, S. (2022). Towards practice research in ethnomusicology. *Ethnomusicology Forum*, 31(1), 10–27. https://doi.org/10.1080/17411912.2021.1964374.

Mogstad, H., & Tse, L.-S. (2018). Decolonizing anthropology: Reflections from Cambridge. *Cambridge Journal of Anthropology*, 36(2), 53–72. https://doi.org/10.3167/cja.2018.360206.

Moore, A. (2010). The track. In A. Bayley, ed., *Recorded Music: Performance, Culture and Technology*. Cambridge: Cambridge University Press, pp. 252–68.

Moore. R. D., ed., (2017). *College Music Curricula for a New Century*. New York: Oxford University Press.

Moore, R. D. (2021). Rethinking the engagement of ethnomusicologists with performance and applied music curricula. In L. F. García Corona & K. Wiens, eds., *Voices of the Field: Pathways in Public Ethnomusicology*. New York: Oxford University Press, pp. 219–37.

Moosavi, L. (2020). The decolonial bandwagon and the dangers of intellectual decolonisation. *International Review of Sociology*, 30, 1–23.

Nelson, R. (2022). Practice as Research in the Arts and Beyond. Principles, Processes, Contexts, Achievements. Palgrave MacMillan.

Nettl, B. (1964). *Theory and Method in Ethnomusicology*. New York: Free Press.

Nettl, B. (2005). *The Study of Ethnomusicology: Thirty-One Issues and Concepts*. Urbana, IL: University of Illinois Press.

Neuman, W. L. (2014). Social Research Methods: Qualitative and Quantitative Approaches. Pearson, p. 7.

Nguyễn, K. T. (2010). Sensing Vietnam: Melodramas of Nation from Colonialism to Market Reform. PhD thesis, Berkeley: University of California.

Nguyen, K. (2012). A personal sorrow: *Cai Luong* and the politics of North and South Vietnam. *Asian Theatre Journal*, 29(1), 255–75.

Nguyen, N. T., & Tangen, D. (2017), Video-stimulated recall in crosscultural research in education: A case study in Vietnam. *International Journal of Research & Method in Education*, 40(5), 445–55. https://doi.org/10.1080/1743727X.2016.1160279.

Nguyễn, T. (2014). No innocent ears: an inter-cultural perspective on the transmission of traditional music. In Östersjö, S. ed., *Spår av musik*. Malmö: Malmö Academy of Music, pp. 255–66.

Nguyễn, T. T. (2019). *The Choreography of Gender in Traditional Vietnamese Music*. PhD thesis, Lund University.

Nguyễn, T. T. (2022). Vietnamese diasporic voices: Exploring yellow music in a liminal space. *VIS – Nordic Journal for Artistic Research*, 8.www.research catalogue.net/view/1513023/1513024/0/1389.

Nguyễn, T. & Östersjö, S. (2019). Arrival cities: Hanoi. In C. Laws, W. Brooks, D. Gorton, et al. eds., *Voices, bodies, practices*. Leuven: Leuven University Press, pp. 235–95.

Nguyễn, T. & Östersjö, S. (2020). Inside the Choreography of Gender. In C. Laws ed., *Performance, Subjectivity, and Experimentation*. Orpheus Institute Series. Leuven: Leuven University Press.

Nguyễn, T. T., & Östersjö, S. (2022). Cultural diplomacy and transculturation through the history of the Vọng Cổ in Vietnam. In D. G. Hebert & J. McCollum, eds., *Ethnomusicology and Cultural Diplomacy*. Lanham, MD: Lexington Books, pp. 181–205.

Norton, B. (2013). Vietnamese popular song in "1968": War, protest and sentimentalism. In B. Kutschke & B. Norton, eds., *Music and Protest in 1968*. Cambridge: Cambridge University Press, pp. 97–118. https://doi.org/10.1017/CBO9781139051682.007.

Ó Briain, L. (2021). Harmonies for the homeland: Traditional music and the politics of intangible cultural heritage on Vietnamese radio. In L. Ó Briain & M. Y. Ong, *Sound Communities in the Asia Pacific: Music, Media, and Technology*. London: Bloomsbury, pp. 73–90. https://doi.org/10.5040/9781501360084.ch-004.

Ó Briain, L. (2021). *Voices of Vietnam: A Century of Radio, Red Music, and Revolution*. New York: Oxford University Press.

Östersjö, S. (2008). Shut Up 'n' Play! Negotiating the Musical Work. PhD thesis, Malmö Academy of Music, Lund University.

Östersjö, S. (2016). Go to Hell: Towards a gesture-based compositional practice. *Contemporary Music Review*, 35(4–5), pp. 475–99. https://doi.org/ 10.1080/07494467.2016.1257625.

Östersjö, S. (2017). Thinking-through-Music: On Knowledge Production, Materiality, Embodiment, and Subjectivity in Artistic Research. In J. Impett ed., *Artistic Research in Music: Discipline and Resistance*. Orpheus Institute Series. Leuven: Leuven University Press, pp. 88–107.

Östersjö, S. (2020). *Listening to the Other*. Leuven: Leuven University Press.

Östersjö, S. (2022). The Vietnamese guitar: Tradition and experiment. In M. Dogantan-Dack, ed., *Rethinking the Musical Instrument*. Newcastle: Cambridge Scholars, pp. 166–93.

Östersjö, S., & Nguyễn, T. (2012). Longing for the past: Musical expression in an inter-cultural perspective. In P. Berry, ed., *If I Were a Drongo Bird: Tankar om längtan, fantasi och skaparkraft tillägnade Håkan Lundström*. Malmö: Malmö Academy of Music, pp. 45–50.

Östersjö, S., & Nguyen, T. (2013). Traditions in transformation: The function of openness in the interaction between musicians in H. Frisk & S. Östersjö, eds., *(re)thinking Improvisation: Artistic Explorations and Conceptual Writing* (Doctoral Studies and Research in Fine and Performing Arts). Malmö: Malmö Academy of Music, pp. 184–201.

Östersjö, Stefan. (2019). "Art Worlds, Voice and Knowledge: thoughts on quality assessment of artistic research outcomes." *ÍMPAR Online journal for artistic research*, 3(2), 60–69 doi: 10.34624/impar.v3i2.14152

Östersjö, S., & Nguyen, T. (2021). Attentive listening in lo-fi soundscapes: Some notes on the development of sound art methodologies in Vietnam. In M. Cobussen & M. Bull, eds., *The Bloomsbury Handbook of Sonic Methodologies*. London: Bloomsbury, pp. 481–95.

Östersjö, S., & Nguyễn, T. T. (2013). Traditions in transformation: The function of openness in the interaction between musicians. In H. Frisk & S. Östersjö, eds., *(re)thinking Improvisation: Artistic Explorations and Conceptual Writing*. Malmö: Malmö Academy of Music, pp. 184–201.

Petitmengin, C. (2006). Describing one's subjective experience in the second person: An interview method for the science of consciousness. *Phenomenology and the Cognitive Sciences*, 5, 229–69. https://doi.org/ 10.1007/s11097-006-9022-2.

Pirie, V. C. (2009). Using video-stimulated recall as a basis for interviews: Some experiences from the field, *Music Education Research*, 11(4), 425–37. https://doi.org/10.1080/14613800903390766.

Rahaim, M. (2017). Otherwise than participation: Unity and alterity in musical encounters. In E. King & C. Waddington, eds., *Music and Empathy*. Abingdon: Routledge, pp. 175–93.

Rao, N. Y. (2014). Cultural boundary and national border: Recent works of Tan Dun, Chen Yi, and Bright Sheng. In H. S. Oh, ed., *Contemporary Music in East Asia*. Seoul: Seoul National University Press, pp. 211–40.

REACT (Rethinking Music Performance in European Higher Education Institutions). (2021). Artistic career in music: Stakeholders requirement report. *UA Editora*. https://doi.org/10.48528/wfq9-4560.

Richardson, W. J. (2018). Understanding Eurocentrism as a structural problem of undone science. In G. K. Bhambra, D. Gebrial, & K. Nisancioglu, eds., *Decolonising the University*. London: Pluto Press, pp. 231–47.

Robinson, D. (2020). *Hungry Listening: Resonant Theory for Indigenous Sound Studies Indigenous Americas* Minneapolis, MN: University of Minnesota Press.

Rose, J. (1994). Communication challenges and role functions of performing groups. *Small Group Research*, 25(3), 411–32.

Rostvall, A.-L., & West, T. (2001). *Interaktion och kunskapsutveckling: en studie av frivillig musikundervisning*. Stockholm: Centrum för musikpedagogisk forskning, Musikhögsk. http://urn.kb.se/resolve?urn=urn:nbn:se:su:diva-73704.

Rostvall, A.-L., & West, T. (2003). Analysis of interaction and learning in instrumental teaching. *Music Education Research*, 5(3), 213–26.

Rostvall, A.-L., & West, T. (2008). Theoretical and methodological perspectives on designing video studies of interaction. *International Journal of Qualitative Methods*, 4(4), 87–108.

Saini, R., & Begum, N. (2020). Demarcation and definition: Explicating the meaning and scope of "decolonisation" in the social and political sciences. *Political Quarterly*, 91(1), 217–21. https://doi.org/10.1111/1467-923X.12797.

Sarath, E. W., Myers, D. E., & Campbell, P. S. (2016). *Redefining Music Studies in an Age of Change: Creativity, Diversity, and Integration*. New York: Routledge.

Schaeffer, P. (2017). *Treatise on Musical Objects: An Essay across Disciplines*. Translated by Christine North and John Dack. Oakland: University of California Press. First published 1966 as *Traité des objets musicaux: Essai interdisciplines* (Paris: Seuil).

SEM. (2020). Open letter from SEM past presidents on racism. Society for Ethnomusicology. www.ethnomusicology.org.

Smith, L. T. (2012). *Decolonizing Methodologies: Research and Indigenous Peoples*. London: Zed Books.

Soliś, T., ed., (2004). *Performing Ethnomusicology: Teaching and Representation in World Music Ensembles.* Berkeley: University of California Press.

Solomon, T. (2012). Where is the postcolonial in ethnomusicology? In S. Nannyonga-Tamusuza & T. Solomon, eds., *Ethnomusicology in East Africa: Perspectives from Uganda and Beyond.* Kampala: Fountain, pp. 216–51.

Stanton, B. (2018). Musicking in the borders toward decolonizing methodologies. *Philosophy of Music Education Review*, 26(1), 4–23.

Stefansdottir, H. S., & Östersjö, S. (2022). Listening and mediation: Of agency and performative responsivity in ecological sound art practices. *Phenomenology & Practice*, 17(1), 116–36. https://doi.org/10.29173/pandpr29464.

Stover, C. (2016). Musical bodies: Corporeality, emergent ubjectivity, and improvisational spaces. *M/C Journal*, **19(1)**. Accessed 29 July 2016. http://journal.media-culture.org.au/.

Tan-Tangbau, S. B. H., & Minh, Q. V. (2021). *Playing Jazz in Socialist Vietnam: Quyền Văn Minh and Jazz in Hà Nội.* Oxford: University Press of Mississippi.

Tan, S. E. (2021). Special issue: Decolonising music and music studies. *Ethnomusicology Forum*, 30(1), 4–8. https://doi.org/10.1080/17411912.2021.1938445.

Taylor, M. M. (1985). Music in the daily experience of grade six children: An interpretive study. *Psychology of Music*, 13(1), 31–39. http://dx.doi.org/10.1177/0305735685131003.

Tenzer, M. (1991). *Balinese Music.* Berkeley, CA: Periplus Editions.

The Six Tones. (2013). *Signal in Noise*, dbcd 157. Malmö: dB Productions

Thomas, D. A. (2018). Decolonizing disciplines. *American Anthropologist*, 120, 393–97. https://doi-org.galanga.hvl.no/10.1111/aman.13102.

Trainor, J. (1975). Significance and development in the Vong Co in South Vietnam. *Asian Music*, 7(1), 50–57. https://doi.org/833927.

Truong-Young, H., & Hogan, T. (2020). Tube housing as dominant system and everyday urban culture of Saigon-Ho Chi Minh City. *Journal of Asian and African Studies*, 55(6), 801–17. https://doi.org/10.1177/0021909620935414.

Unander-Scharin, Å. (2008). *Mänsklig mekanik och besjälade maskiner: koreografiska perspektiv på mänskliga kvaliteter i kroppars rörelse.* [Doctoral dissertation, Luleå University of Technology, Department of Arts, Communication and Education, Music and Dance].

Utz, C. (2021). *Musical Composition in the Context of Globalization: New Perspectives on Music History of the 20th and 21st Century.* Bielefeld: Transcript.

Verbeek, P.-P. (2008). Cyborg intentionality: Rethinking the phenomenology of human–technology relations. *Phenomenology and the Cognitive Sciences*, 7, 387–95. https://doi.org/10.1007/s11097-008-9099-x.

Vermersch, P. (1999). Introspection as practice. *Journal of Consciousness Studies*, 6(2–3), 17–42.

West, T. (2014). Music and designed sound. In C. Jewitt, ed., *The Routledge Handbook of Multimodal Analysis, 2nd ed*. London: Routledge, pp. 410–18.

West, T., & Rostvall, A.-L. (2003). A study of interaction and learning in instrumental teaching. *International Journal of Music Education*, 40, 16–29.

Yamauchi, F. (2019). Contemplating East Asian music history in regional and global contexts. In T. Janz & C.-C. Yang, eds., *Decentering Musical Modernity: Perspectives on East Asian and European Music History*, Bielefeld: Transcript, pp. 207–45.

Žižek, S. (2011). How to Read Lacan. London: Granta Books.

Cambridge Elements ≡

Elements in Twenty-First Century Music Practice

Simon Zagorski-Thomas

London College of Music, University of West London

Simon Zagorski-Thomas is a Professor at the London College of Music (University of West London, UK) and founded and runs the 21st Century Music Practice Research Network. He is series editor for the Cambridge Elements series and Bloomsbury book series on 21st Century Music Practice. He is ex-chairman and co-founder of the Association for the Study of the Art of Record Production. He is a composer, sound engineer and producer and is, currently, writing a monograph on practical musicology. His books include *Musicology of Record Production* (2014; winner of the 2015 IASPM Book Prize), *The Art of Record Production: an Introductory Reader for a New Academic Field* co-edited with Simon Frith (2012), the *Bloomsbury Handbook of Music Production* co-edited with Andrew Bourbon (2020) and the *Art of Record Production: Creative Practice in the Studio* co-edited with Katia Isakoff, Serge Lacasse and Sophie Stévance (2020).

About the Series

Elements in Twenty-First Century Music Practice has developed out of the 21st Century Music Practice Research Network, which currently has around 250 members in 30 countries and is dedicated to the study of what Christopher Small termed musicking – the process of making and sharing music rather than the output itself. Obviously this exists at the intersection of ethnomusicology, performance studies, and practice pedagogy / practice-led-research in composition, performance, recording, production, musical theatre, music for screen and other forms of multi-media musicking. The generic nature of the term '21st Century Music Practice' reflects the aim of the series to bring together all forms of music into a larger discussion of current practice and to provide a platform for research about any musical tradition or style. It embraces everything from hip-hop to historically informed performance and K-pop to Inuk throat singing.

Cambridge Elements ≡

Elements in Twenty-First Century Music Practice

Elements in the Series

The Marks of a Maestro: Annotating Mozart's "Jupiter" Symphony
Raymond Holden and Stephen Mould

Chinese Street Music: Complicating Musical Community
Samuel Horlor

Reimagine to Revitalise: New Approaches to Performance Practices Across Cultures
Charulatha Mani

A Philosophy of Playing Drum Kit
Gareth Dylan Smith

Shared Listenings: Methods for Transcultural Musicianship and Research
Stefan Östersjö, Nguyễn Thanh Thủy, David G. Hebert, and Henrik Frisk

Printed in the United States
by Baker & Taylor Publisher Services